A Student's Guide to GCSE Music

for the **Edexcel** Specification

by

John Arkell and David Bowman

Edited by
Lucien Jenkins and Abigail Walmsley

Rhinegold Publishing Ltd
241 Shaftesbury Avenue
London WC2H 8TF
Telephone: 01832 270333
Fax: 01832 275560
www.rhinegold.co.uk

Rhinegold Music Study Guides
(series editor: Paul Terry)

A Student's Guide to GCSE Music for the Edexcel Specification
Listening Tests for Students (Books 1 and 2): Edexcel GCSE Music Specification

A Student's Guide to AS Music for the Edexcel Specification
A Student's Guide to A2 Music for the Edexcel Specification
Listening Tests for Students (Books 1 and 2): Edexcel AS Music Specification
Listening Tests for Students (Books 1 and 2): Edexcel A2 Music Specification

Similar books have been produced for the AQA and OCR Music Specifications. Also available are:
A Student's Guide to GCSE Music for the WJEC Specification (separate English and Welsh language versions)
A Student's Guide to Music Technology for the Edexcel AS and A2 Specification
Listening Tests for Students: Edexcel Music Technology AS and A2 Music Specification

The following books are designed to support all GCSE and GCE music courses:
A Student's Guide to Composing (Book 1 for GCSE and Book 2 for A-level Music)
A Student's Guide to Harmony and Counterpoint (for AS and A2 Music)

Other Rhinegold Study Guides
Students' Guides to AS and A2 Drama and Theatre Studies for the AQA and Edexcel Specifications
Students' Guides to AS and A2 Performance Studies for the OCR Specification
Students' Guides to AS and A2 Religious Studies for the AQA, Edexcel and OCR Specifications

Rhinegold Publishing also publishes Classical Music, Classroom Music, Early Music Today, Music Teacher,
Opera Now, Piano, The Singer, British and International Music Yearbook, British Performing Arts Yearbook,
Music Education Yearbook, Rhinegold Dictionary of Music in Sound.

First published 2002 in Great Britain by
Rhinegold Publishing Ltd
241 Shaftesbury Avenue
London WC2H 8TF
Telephone: 01832 270333
Fax: 01832 275560
www.rhinegold.co.uk
Reprinted 2003, 2004, 2005

© Rhinegold Publishing Ltd 2002,2005

You should always check the current requirements of the examination, since these may change.
Copies of the Edexcel Specification may be obtained from Edexcel Examinations at
Edexcel Publications, Adamsway, Mansfield, Notts, NG18 4FN
Telephone 01623 467467, Fax 01623 450481, Email publications@linneydirect.com
See also the Edexcel website at www.edexcel.org.uk

A Student's Guide to GCSE Music for the Edexcel Specification
British Library Cataloguing in Publication Data.
A catalogue record for this book is available from the British Library.

ISBN 1-904226-01-9

Printed in Great Britain by WPG Group Ltd

Contents

The authors

David Bowman was for 20 years director of music at Ampleforth College where he still teaches. He was a chief examiner for the University of London Schools Examination Board (now Edexcel) from 1982 to 1998. He now spends more time with his family, horses and dogs.

David Bowman's publications include the *London Anthology of Music* (University of London Schools Examination Board, 1986), *Sound Matters* (co-authored with Bruce Cole, Schott, 1989), *Aural Matters* (co-authored with Paul Terry, Schott, 1993), *Aural Matters in Practice* (co-authored with Paul Terry, Schott, 1994), *Analysis Matters* (Rhinegold, Volume 1 1997, Volume 2 1998) and numerous analytical articles for *Music Teacher*. He is a contributor to the *Collins Music Encyclopedia* (2000) edited by Stanley Sadie and author of the *Rhinegold Dictionary of Music in Sound* (Rhinegold Publishing 2002).

John Arkell is head of academic music and organist at Oundle School. He has taught music at GCSE and A Level for 12 years, for eight of which he has been an examiner for Edexcel at Advanced Level. John is now the principal examiner and moderator for the new Edexcel GCSE qualification. In addition to his specific responsibility for the composition component of Paper 2, he is also involved with the setting and revising of questions for the Paper 3 examination in Listening and Appraising.

He has also been active as an arranger and editor for Fentone Music Publications and his most recent publication is a set of organ pieces entitled *The Oundle Organ Series*. Although John has worked with David Bowman in the past as an examiner, this is their first writing venture together.

Acknowledgements

The authors would like to thank David Adams, Nicola Grist and Adrian Hooper of Edexcel, Dr Julia Winterson of Peters Edition, Hallam Bannister, Ann Barkway, Andy Channing, Bruce Cole, Laura Davey, Edward Dudley Hughes, Emily Keeler (Sewa Beats), Robert Kwami, Robert Mason, Paul Terry and Adrian York for their advice and support during the preparation of this guide.

Nevertheless if any errors have been made it is only right to state that these are the responsibilities of the authors.

Abbreviations

GAM: *The GCSE Anthology of Music* (ed) Julia Winterson, Peters Edition Ltd, ISBN 1-901507-78-5

NAM: *The New Anthology of Music* (ed) Julia Winterson, Peters Edition Ltd, ISBN 1-901507-03-3 (for Edexcel AS and A2 Music)

RDMS: *The Rhinegold Dictionary of Music in Sound* David Bowman, Rhinegold, ISBN 0-946890-87-0

SM: Sound Matters David Bowman and Bruce Cole, Schott and Co Ltd, ISBN 0-946535-14-0

Introduction

This is a guide specially written for pupils studying for the Edexcel GCSE in music. You're still going to need to go to your lessons: we are offering you some extra help, not a substitute for what your teachers have to offer. First, here's an outline of what you should be doing.

You will have to perform, compose, and listen and appraise. This will involve being able to:

◆ play and/or sing an individual part with technical control, expression, interpretation and, where appropriate, a sense of ensemble (performing)

◆ create and develop musical ideas in relation to a set of detailed instructions (composing)

◆ analyse and evaluate music using musical terminology (appraising).

Your teachers are going to want you to make the most of your own musical interests but they will also introduce you to new styles of music. The world you live in contains many different cultures. Your two-year GCSE course aims to reflect this so you will study various kinds of music, including:

◆ classical music (Areas of Study 1 and 2)

◆ popular music (Area of Study 3)

◆ world music (Area of Study 4).

At the end of the course your examiners will want to see that you can:

◆ understand a range of different kinds of music

◆ make judgements about musical quality

◆ think creatively and critically.

GCSE music

Performing accounts for 30% of your GCSE

(a) Solo performance	You will perform **one** piece	15%
(b) Performing during the course	You will perform or direct **two** other pieces. These must include your Composition 1 and, if that is not an ensemble piece, a work that is for ensemble.	15%

Performing

Composing	*Composing accounts for 30% of your GCSE*		
	(a) Composition 1	One composition, written to a set brief, based on one of the four Areas of Study	15%
	(b) Composition 2	Another composition, written to a set brief, but based on a **different** Area of Study.	15%
Listening and appraising	*Listening and appraising accounts for 40% of your GCSE*		
	Listening paper	A 1½-hour written paper containing questions based on **all four Areas of Study**.	40%

Areas of Study

The four Areas of Study form the backbone of your GCSE Music and connect the **Performing**, **Composing** and **Listening** elements in your course. It will also be possible to make links between different Areas of Study. For example in your study of the repeated patterns of ground-bass (Area of Study 1), comparisons can be made with the 12-bar blues (Area of Study 3); you will find links between gamelan and Lou Harrison (Area of Study 3) and John Cage and Stockhausen (Area of Study 2).

The four Areas of Study themselves cover a wide range of music from about 1600 to the present day including classical and popular music, and music from around the world. Each Area of Study contains four topics. Remember that you are encouraged to use what you learn in the Areas of Study not just in the Listening and Appraising paper but in the Performing and Composing papers as well.

You'll need a good knowledge of the stylistic features of the four topics in each Area of Study. We'll talk about this in individual chapters, but for now just note that a question set in the Listening Paper on ternary form (for example) could come from any period, so a broad understanding of the conventions of each period is vital.

The Listening Paper

In the exam you will have to answer questions about a number of extracts of music played on CD. Each extract will be repeated at least once, but you will not be given a score of the music. You may be asked to identify instruments, styles and technical features, to describe and compare the music (using technical terms) and to show how it relates to features of the works you have studied.

Rhinegold produces workbooks and accompanying CDs that provide practice material for Edexcel GCSE listening tests: *Listening Tests for Students Book 1 (Edexcel GCSE Music Specification)* and *Listening Tests for Students Book 2 (Edexcel GCSE Music Specification)* by Ian Burton.

These exam extracts will be taken from the four Areas of Study, **but they are most unlikely to come from specific pieces that you have studied in *GAM*.** The works we discuss in this book (including those in *GAM*) will introduce you to important features of the music in each Area of Study, but in order to do well in the exam you will need plenty of practise in answering questions on similar but unfamiliar music. On page 106 we have provided some sample questions that will help show you what to expect.

Understanding music

This chapter covers some important terms and concepts that you will encounter during your course. Some of the points, particularly on keys and chords, may seem very difficult at first so don't try to work through the entire chapter in one go – use it as a reference source whenever you need to. Don't forget that the purpose of music theory is not to give you things to learn for homework but to help you become a better listener, performer and composer.

You will undoubtedly encounter many musical terms that are new to you. These will make much more sense if you understand the *sounds* to which they refer. Don't just rely on learning definitions, but play or sing the examples and use them in your own composing. Understanding musical terminology will help you convey to fellow musicians (even examiners!) complex ideas in just a word or two, rather than having to use long descriptions. But remember that musical terminology must be understood thoroughly and used correctly if you are to make sense.

Clefs

You will probably be familiar with the **treble clef**. Its symbol (𝄞) developed from an elaborate letter G which wraps around the line of the stave that represents the pitch G above middle C.

You will also encounter the **bass clef**. Its symbol (𝄢) developed from a letter F which wraps around the line of the stave that represents the pitch F below middle C.

The treble clef is used for melody instruments such as the flute, oboe, clarinet, saxophone, trumpet, horn, violin and recorder, as well as for treble and alto voices. The bass clef is used for bass voices and bass instruments such as the bassoon, trombone, tuba, cello and double bass. Keyboard instruments and the harp use both clefs.

The **vocal tenor clef** is easy to understand. It looks the same as a treble clef but with a small figure *8* at the bottom. This indicates that the music sounds an octave lower than the equivalent treble clef notes. It is used for tenor voices (hence its name) and for lead-guitar parts. Sometimes these parts are written in the normal treble clef, it being taken for granted that tenor singers and guitarists know that their part sounds an octave lower than written.

The symbol for the C clef (𝄡) developed from a letter C which wraps around the line of the stave that represents middle C. It can appear on the middle line of the stave, in which case it is known as the alto clef. Viola parts use this version of the C clef. It can also appear on the fourth line up of the stave, in which case it is known as the tenor clef. The tenor clef is used for the higher notes of the cello, double bass, bassoon and trombone. You will not need to become expert in reading the C clef unless you choose to use it in your compositions.

The examples *right* show the first three notes of *Three Blind Mice* in all five of these clefs. Notice that all five end on middle C and they all sound exactly the same. The last stave in the example uses a percussion clef. It doesn't indicate pitches at all, but it allows a stave to be used for a variety of drum-kit sounds.

To understand this chapter you will need to be able to read simple music notation. If you find this difficult try to spend some time early in the course getting yourself up to speed. There are many books on music notation and theory – your teacher will be able to suggest one that is appropriate. There are also websites and CD-Roms on the subject and these often allow you to test yourself as you go. The best way of all though, is to identify gaps in your knowledge and then ask your teacher for help. They won't mind – in fact they will be delighted if you are interested in improving your skills. And your teacher can explain things in the way you are most likely to understand if you find a concept hard to grasp. Remember that the best way to practise music-reading skills, and to explore new music, is to do as much sight-reading as you can manage.

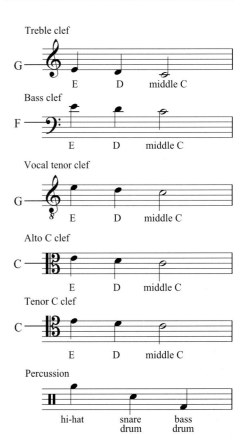

Major scales and major keys

Scales are one of the main building-blocks in many types of music. We may not enjoy playing them, but they are essential in building up an understanding of how music works.

'Semi' means 'half', so a semitone is half a tone.

An interval is the distance between two pitches. The smallest interval normally used in western music is a semitone. On the keyboard diagram *below* there is a semitone between notes 1 and 2, and another semitone between notes 2 and 3. The interval between notes 1 and 3 is therefore two semitones, or a tone.

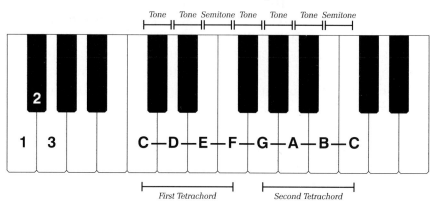

Now look at the scale of C major shown on this diagram. There is no black note between E and F, or between B and C. This is because these notes are already only a semitone apart.

Can you see the pattern of intervals in this scale? It starts with a group of four notes (known as a tetrachord) that are separated by the intervals tone–tone–semitone. And it ends with another group of four notes in exactly the same pattern. The last note of the first tetrachord and the first note of the second are a tone apart. So the entire eight-note scale makes the pattern:

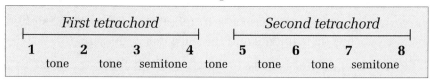

It may seem complicated but once you understand the pattern you can construct every major scale there is!

Let's put theory into practice and use the formula to construct a major scale starting on G. The first tetrachord will be G–A–B–C, which happens to be the same as the second tetrachord of C major (see *left*). We know that the other tetrachord must start a tone above the last note of the first tetrachord. To keep to the invariable tone–tone–semitone pattern it will have to consist of the notes D–E–F♯–G.

The important difference between the notes of C major and G major is that the former uses F♮ while the latter uses F♯. Keys which have most of their notes in common like this are described as being closely related.

Now try constructing a scale of D major. It begins with the second tetrachord of G major, shown left (D–E–F♯–G) and it ends with the tetrachord A–B–C♯–D. This scale is closely related to G major (only one pitch, C♯, is different) but less closely related to C major (where two pitches, F♯ and C♯, are different).

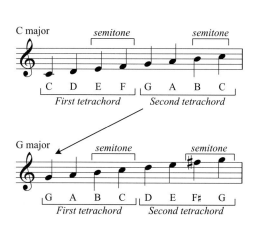

Follow the pattern one more time and write out a major scale starting on A. You should find that this time you need three sharps. Do you notice that every time you start a new scale on the fifth note of the previous scale, it needs one more sharp?

Now try writing out the major scale that starts on the fourth note of C major (F). In order to maintain our usual pattern you should end up with the scale of F major shown *right*. We can see that it is closely related to C major because both keys have all notes except one (Bb) in common. Repeat the process by starting a scale on the fourth note of F major (Bb), and you should find that the new scale needs two flats (Bb and Eb). You have probably guessed by now – every time you start a new scale on the fourth note of the previous scale, it needs one more flat.

Rather than writing a sharp or flat before each note that needs one it is more convenient to use a key signature at the start of each stave to indicate the sharps or flats required.

There are 12 possible major keys in all, and you can see their relationships in the following diagram. Keys next to each other in the circle are closely related. Notice that, at the top of the circle, the notes in the key of F♯ major (six sharps) sound the same as the notes in the key of G♭ major (six flats). They are said to be enharmonic equivalents, which means that they sound the same but are written differently.

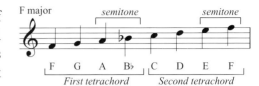

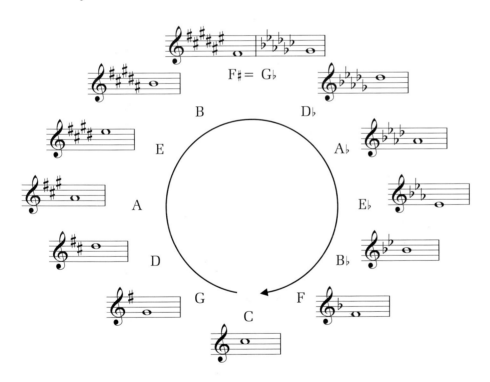

Notice that if you go round the circle clockwise from C major you add a sharp for each new key until you get to six sharps. It is then more sensible to use flats – and you must deduct a flat for each new key until you get back to C major.

When you write out a key signature the sharps or flats are always used in the fixed order shown above. If you need to use the bass clef, follow the order given in the example shown *right*.

Scale degrees

It is often more convenient to refer not to individual note names but to the function of each note in a scale. For example the first note of a major (or minor) scale is always the key note, or tonic, whatever key the music is in. Here are the technical names for each degree of the scale – Roman numerals are often used instead of the technical names:

1 Tonic	2 Super- tonic	3 Mediant	4 Sub- dominant	5 Dominant	6 Sub- mediant	7 Leading note	8 Tonic
I	**II**	**III**	**IV**	**V**	**VI**	**VII**	**I**

Earlier we saw how one of the most closely related keys to a tonic is the one a 5th higher – so you won't be surprised to see that V is called the dominant. In the example below we can see that the dominant note of G is D. Similarly, the dominant key of G major is D major.

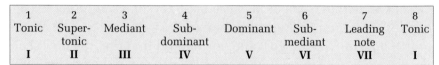

G major

Tonic — Supertonic — Mediant — Subdominant — Dominant — Submediant — Leading-note — Tonic

I   II   III   IV   V   VI   VII   I

? Test yourself on major scales and keys

1. Write out the scale of E♭ major in the treble clef. Which note is the dominant of E♭ major?

2. Write out the scale of A major in the bass clef. Which note is the subdominant of A major?

Minor scales and minor keys

Minor keys are sometimes misleadingly described as sad and major keys as happy. Fast music in a minor key can sound brilliant, stormy or angry, just as slow music in a major key can sound tragic or nostalgic. If asked to identify a key as being major or minor in a listening test you will need to listen very carefully to the relationship between notes and not rely on simplistic descriptions of this kind.

Paired with every major key is a minor key with the same key signature. This **relative minor** is another key that is closely related to the original tonic. It always starts on the submediant (sixth note) of its matching major key. So the relative minor of C major starts on A and is called A minor. Instead of counting up six steps to the submediant to find the starting note, you may prefer to think of it as two scale steps below the tonic:

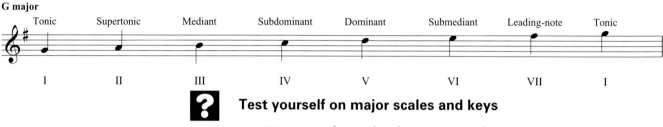

C major   Relative minor of C major is A minor

I   II   III   IV   V   VI   or   I   VII   VI

We can say that A minor is the relative minor of C major, or we can say that C major is the relative major of A minor. The starting note (or tonic) of all other minor keys is worked out in exactly the same way. So, what is the relative minor of each of the following keys: G major, D major, F major, B♭ major, A major, E♭ major?

Minor scales come in several different versions. The easiest one to start with is what is known in pop and jazz as the natural minor. It uses exactly the same notes as its relative major, but because it starts on a different tonic, the relationship between the notes in the scale is different:

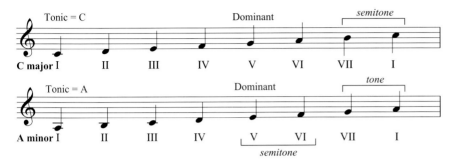

This different relationship is most obvious at the end of the scale. Play or sing several scales of C major, each time stopping on note VII. You will undoubtedly feel that the scale sounds incomplete unless the last note rises a semitone to finish on C, the tonic. This tendency is so strong that it gives note VII its technical name of leading-note – the note that needs to lead to the tonic.

The natural minor scale ends with an interval of a tone, and so doesn't display this tendency to the same extent. Repeat the experiment with the second example above, stopping on VII, and you will find that the need for it to rise to the tonic is less strongly felt.

This is the main reason why different forms of the minor scale have evolved. The natural minor does not convey a strong sense of tonality (by which is meant a sense of key in which the tonic is the most important note). In order to establish a strong sense of key, the minor scale needs to end with the same rising semitone between VII and I that is found in major keys. The easy way to achieve this is to raise note VII by a semitone, but this then creates a rather odd-sounding interval between notes VI and VII:

If you have had to prepare scales for exams you may recognise that the example *left* is known as the harmonic minor scale – it is better suited for harmonising music than for use in melodies because of the awkward interval between notes VI and VII.

To avoid this awkward interval, note VI is also often raised by a semitone, giving the following version of a minor scale:

You may recognise that this example comes from the melodic minor scale, which is better suited for melody writing. It has the pattern shown here when ascending but it uses the natural-minor scale pattern when descending.

In a minor-key piece you may thus find notes VI and VII in both normal and raised versions:

Vivaldi, Op.3 No.8

However the raised version of the leading note followed by the tonic (shown bracketed above) is needed to convey a firm sense of minor tonality, and the presence of this pattern is a clear indicator that the key is minor.

Notice that raising the pitch of notes VI and VII does not always mean using a sharp. If either of these notes is normally flat, then you will need a natural, not a sharp, to raise its pitch by a semitone:

C minor: I   II   III   IV   V   VI   VII   I

Try to build-up speed and accuracy in recognising keys, scales and the degrees of the scale – it will help you understand later topics, particularly chords, very much more easily.

? Test yourself on minor scales and keys

1. Name the relative minor of F major and state the pitch of its raised leading note. ....

2. Write out the scale of G minor in the treble clef, using the raised form of the sixth and seventh degrees of this scale.

3. Name the key of the following passage of music: ....

Vivaldi, Op.3 No.2

Other scales and modes

Pentatonic scale starting on C

1   2   3   5   6   1

The **pentatonic scale** is a five-note scale found in folk music in many different parts of the world. In its most common form it uses notes 1–2–3–5–6–1 of the major scale (see *left*). If you play a scale on just the black notes of a keyboard, starting on F♯, you will hear the pentatonic scale in F♯.

The pentatonic scale is very useful when you first start composing because, since it doesn't include any semitones, it is possible to combine melodic lines with simple drone accompaniments without creating harsh dissonances.

Unlike the pentatonic scale, the **chromatic scale** consists entirely of semitones, 12 of them to the octave:

Chromatic scale

The **whole-tone scale**, as you might guess, proceeds entirely in steps of a tone:

Whole-tone scale

A **mode** is simply a set of notes. The major scale is one kind of mode and the natural minor scale that we saw on page 12 is another – indeed, it is the same as the aeolian mode printed *right*. This example shows three of the most common modes. At first sight they may look like major scales, but the significant difference is the relationship of the notes within the mode. Notice that none ends with a semitone between its last two notes – one of the characteristic features of a major scale. For GCSE you will not be required to distinguish between the different types of mode, but you might be expected to recognise that a passage is modal.

Aeolian mode

Dorian mode

Mixolydian mode

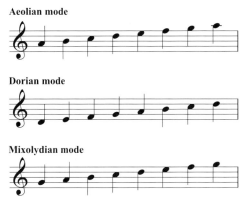

Intervals

We have already learnt that an interval is the distance between two notes. If the two notes occur simultaneously they form a harmonic interval. If they occur in succession they form a melodic interval, either ascending or descending. All are described in the same way, by counting the letter names from the lower note to the higher note. Always count the lower note as 1. All three of the intervals shown *right* are 5ths.

However describing intervals by number alone is insufficient. For instance, the interval from D to F is a 3rd – but so is the interval from D to F♯ and they are clearly not the same. We need to add a description of the 'quality' of the interval in order to be more precise.

To do this, imagine that the lower note of the interval is the key note (or tonic) of a major scale. If the upper note falls within that scale the interval will be named as follows:

| (perfect) unison | major 2nd | major 3rd | perfect 4th | perfect 5th | major 6th | major 7th | (perfect) octave | major 9th |

In every major and minor scale, you'll find that the intervals between the tonic and fourth, fifth and octave degrees above are called 'perfect'.

If the interval is one semitone smaller than a major interval, it is a minor interval. That gives us the following possibilities:

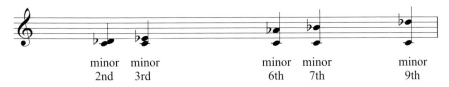

| minor 2nd | minor 3rd | minor 6th | minor 7th | minor 9th |

The minor 2nd sounds the same as a semitone and the major 2nd sounds the same as a tone. Notice how you have to stagger the note heads when writing these small intervals on a single stave.

If an interval is one semitone smaller than a minor or perfect interval, it is diminished. And if an interval is one semitone larger than a major or perfect interval, it is augmented:

| major 7th | minor 7th | diminished 7th | perfect 5th | diminished 5th | perfect 4th | augmented 4th | major 2nd | augmented 2nd |

The diminished 5th and the augmented 4th sound the same when heard in isolation. Both consist of an interval of three tones, and each is therefore often called a **tritone**.

Notice that you can alter the quality of an interval by changing either of its notes. The diminished 7th in the above example is a semitone smaller than the minor 7th because its lower note has been raised by a semitone.

Naming intervals: a summary

First work out the number of the interval. Next decide if the upper note is in the major scale in which the lower note is the tonic. If it is, the interval will be major or perfect. If not, the following rules usually help:

    If the interval is a semitone smaller than a major interval, it is minor
    If the interval is a semitone larger than a major or perfect interval, it is augmented
    If the interval is a semitone smaller than a minor or perfect interval, it is diminished.

One of the most confusing things about naming intervals is the fact that minor intervals occur in major keys, and major intervals occur in minor keys. Let's see how this works in practice with the examples shown *left*.

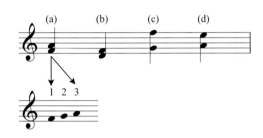

First work out the number of the interval, remembering to count the lower note as 1. Interval (a) is a 3rd (F=1, G=2, A=3). Next imagine the lower note (F) to be the tonic. Does the upper note (A) occur in the key of F major? Yes! So this is a major 3rd.

Example (b) is also a 3rd. Imagine the lower note (D) to be the tonic. Does the upper note (F) occur in the key of D major? No! The third note in D major is F♯, but here we have F♮ – so interval (b) is a semitone less than a major 3rd. It is a minor 3rd.

Now work out interval (c). The lower note is G. Does the upper note (F) occur in G major? If it doesn't, this cannot be a major interval. What interval is it? Work out interval (d) for yourself.

 Test yourself on intervals

Write the named harmonic interval by writing a note *above* each of the following notes.

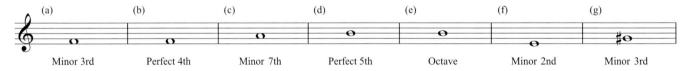

(a)	(b)	(c)	(d)	(e)	(f)	(g)
Minor 3rd	Perfect 4th	Minor 7th	Perfect 5th	Octave	Minor 2nd	Minor 3rd

Triads

The simplest type of chord is the **triad**. It consists of three pitches: the note on which the chord is based (the **root**), along with a 3rd and 5th above it. Here are the triads on each note of C major:

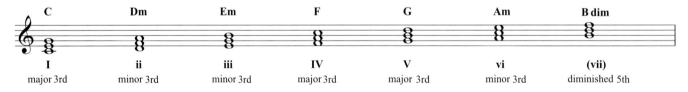

C	Dm	Em	F	G	Am	B dim
I	ii	iii	IV	V	vi	(vii)
major 3rd	minor 3rd	minor 3rd	major 3rd	major 3rd	minor 3rd	diminished 5th

Triads can be described by using the technical names or the Roman numerals that are used for naming the degrees of the scale. For instance, in the key of C major the dominant chord (chord V) is simply the triad on the dominant note (G).

Upper-case Roman numerals (ie I, II, etc) are often used to indicate major triads while lower-case Roman numerals (ie i, ii, etc) can be used to indicate minor triads.

Look carefully at the interval between the root and third of each chord. In chords I, IV and V the middle note is a major 3rd above the root. These are therefore major chords, and are known as the three primary triads. In chords ii, iii and vi the middle note is a minor 3rd above the root. These are known as minor chords.

The interval between the root and top note is a perfect 5th in every triad except vii. Here the outer interval is a diminished 5th and this triad is therefore known as a diminished triad.

In pop and jazz it is more usual to notate chords by writing the letter name of the root above the stave. A single capital letter indicates a major chord. A lower case 'm' after a capital letter indicates a minor chord, while 'dim' indicates a diminished triad.

The notes of a chord can be positioned in any octave, with any spacing and with notes duplicated. All of the chords shown *right* are G major – even the last one can be assumed to be G major, despite the fact that one of the notes (the 5th, D) is omitted.

Notice that the root of the triad (G) is the lowest note of all five chords in this example. When, as here, the root is also the bass note the chord is said to be in **root position**.

Inversions

If a chord is arranged so that the root is *not* the lowest note it is said to be inverted. If the 3rd is in the bass the triad is said to be in first inversion. This is indicated by adding the letter 'b' to the appropriate Roman numeral (see *right*: a root-position triad should have the letter 'a' after the Roman numeral, but it is usually omitted). You may also see a first inversion expressed as $\frac{6}{3}$, indicating that the upper two notes are a 6th and a 3rd above the bass.

If the 5th is in the bass the triad is said to be in second inversion and this is indicated by adding the letter 'c' to the appropriate Roman numeral. You may see a second inversion expressed as $\frac{6}{4}$, indicating that the upper notes are a 6th and a 4th above the bass.

It should now be clear that however the upper notes of a chord are arranged, the bass note is especially important. This is also true if you use chord symbols other than Roman numerals. If the bass note is not the root, write an oblique stroke after the chord symbol and then name the bass note required: eg C/E indicates a chord of C major with E in the bass (in other words, a first inversion).

More elaborate chords can be formed by adding a 7th above the root – you will often see chords V and II embellished in this way, as shown *right*. If you add a diminished 7th to chord VII you will form a dramatic chord known as a diminished seventh.

It is also possible to add other notes to triads (such as 2nds or 9ths) and to make chromatic alterations to one or more of the notes of the triad. However while such techniques are well worth exploring when composing, they are beyond the requirements of GCSE.

Melodic decoration

If melodies only used notes from the current chord they would sound very dull, so basic harmony notes are frequently enlivened with various types of melodic decoration. These often create a momentary dissonance (ie a clash) with the underlying harmony.

These decorative (or 'unessential') notes may be **diatonic**, which means they use notes from the prevailing key, or they may be **chromatic**, meaning that they use notes from outside the prevailing key. And, although we have called this section melodic decoration, these embellishments may occur in the melody, bass or an inner part.

An **auxiliary note** lies a tone or a semitone above or below a harmony note and alternates with it. A **passing note** moves by step between two harmony notes that are a third apart. Passing notes normally occur on weak beats. If they occur on strong beats they will be much more obviously dissonant and are then known as accented passing notes.

An **appoggiatura** is a dissonance that is approached by a leap. The tension created is released when the appoggiatura 'resolves' by moving to a harmony note.

A **suspension** starts with a consonant note which is then sustained or repeated (ie suspended) over a change of harmony, causing a discord. The discord then resolves to a harmony note, usually by moving downwards by step. In most cases the suspension actually replaces one of the harmony notes. For instance in the example *left*, the normal 3rd of a C-major chord (E) has been temporarily replaced by F, a 4th above C. In pop and jazz, suspensions are often treated as chords in their own right and are notated with a separate chord symbol ($C^{sus\,4}$ in this case).

Figuration

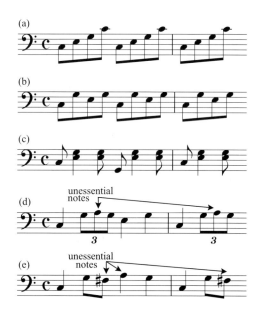

If chords were always used as plain blocks of notes music would sound very dull. Even in a simple accompanied melody composers usually make the accompaniment more interesting by devising patterns from the chord notes. These patterns are known as figures, and can be adapted to fit changes in the chords. The example *left* shows just five ways of devising a figure from a C-major chord. Pattern (a) is a simple arpeggio figure, while (b) is a broken-chord figure known as an Alberti bass (named after a composer who over-used this type of figuration). The syncopation in pattern (c) gives this figure a more urgent feel. Patterns (d) and (e) both include unessential notes.

Motifs, phrases and cadences

A **motif** is a short melodic or rhythmic idea that is distinctive enough to maintain its identity despite being changed in various ways. It is often the basic cell from which much longer musical ideas are constructed, as in this example by Mozart:

The opening motif (x) features a rhythm (♪♩|♩) and a falling semitone. First it is repeated exactly, then it is repeated and extended by an upward leap and a rest. Next it is adapted so that the third note falls (x^1). This variant is then treated in **sequence** (which means the immediate repetition of an idea at a different pitch). The last appearance is again extended to match the rhythm (but not the rising leap) of the first extension. The entire **phrase** quoted above is then repeated in sequence a step lower, creating a perfectly balanced pair of phrases.

The phrase above begins on the last beat of a bar. An opening on a weak beat like this is known as an anacrusis. It means that the music starts with an incomplete bar and the final bar of the example is shortened to balance. The example thus contains 16 beats in all and we can still refer to it as being a four-bar phrase, even though it doesn't fit into four complete bars. Notice how bars are numbered when there is an anacrusic start – bar 1 is the first *complete* bar.

Phrases often end with a cadence – a point of repose, rather like punctuation in a sentence. The perfect cadence (chords V–I) gives a sense of completion, rather like a full stop at the end of a sentence. The imperfect cadence (an ending on chord V) sounds open and incomplete – more like a comma after a phrase in a sentence:

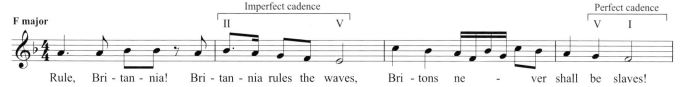

Note that chord V in an imperfect cadence can be preceded by any suitable chord (I, II or IV are the most usual).

Two other cadences you may encounter are illustrated *right*. The plagal cadence consists of chords IV–I and is often associated with a sung 'Amen' in church music. The interrupted cadence begins with chord V (or V⁷) like a perfect cadence, but it ends with any chord other than I – in other words, the expected perfect cadence is interrupted by an unexpected chord.

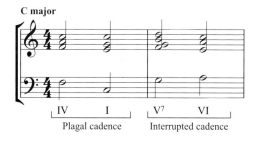

Modulation

The perfect cadence, particularly in the form V^7–I, has an important role in defining the key. Chord V^7 includes the leading note, which tends to want to rise to the tonic in chord I, while the seventh of chord V^7 tends to want to fall to the third in chord I. These two chords totally define a key. Look at the melody shown *right*, which clearly outlines a perfect cadence. The chord of C^7 includes B♭, so the key must be a flat key, but it also includes E♮. There are only two keys with this combination, F major and F minor. And when the 7th (B♭) drops to A♮ in the tonic chord we know that the key cannot be F minor – it can only be F major.

When you see accidentals in a passage of music, they can have any of the following functions:

◆ they may be the sixth and/or seventh notes of a minor key
◆ they may indicate that the music has modulated (changed key)
◆ they may be chromatic notes which have no effect on the key.

The role of the perfect cadence in defining key will enable us to differentiate between these different functions of accidentals. Look at the following melody by Sousa:

When you see an accidental, ask yourself if it might be a leading note – if it is, the tonic will be a semitone higher and you would expect to see a perfect cadence in this key. So, the presence of G# might suggest the key of A minor, and F# might suggest G minor. But there are no perfect cadences in either of these keys.

There are only two different chords, C⁷ and F, and these make a clear perfect cadence in F major in bars 6–7.

Next look at this minuet by Mozart. It also starts in F major, as confirmed by the perfect cadence (C⁷–F) in bars 3–4. The first accidental is B♮ in bar 5. Is this merely chromatic or does it signify a modulation? As always, test to see if it is a leading note (eg of C major) by looking for a perfect cadence in this new key. This time there are perfect cadences in the new key, in bars 5–6 (G⁷–C) and again in bars 7–8 (G–C). So B♮ is not a chromatic note – the music does indeed modulate to the key of C major.

Remember, for a modulation to take place you should expect to see not only accidentals that reflect the new key, but also a perfect cadence in the new key.

Performing for GCSE music

What you have to do

The performing paper accounts for 30% of the marks for GCSE Music. It has two parts:

✦ Solo Performing is alloted 15% of the total GCSE mark and for this you will have to present one piece

✦ Performing During the Course also accounts for 15% of the total mark and for this you will need to present two other pieces.

You are required to perform a solo piece on an instrument of your choice. The music can be in any style or tradition. But it is obviously sensible to choose a piece that has plenty of variety and that will show your skills to their best advantage.

Although Edexcel gives no minimum time limit, *your piece should not exceed five minutes*. Remember though, if your piece is very brief, it might be hard to assess your performing standard accurately. You are allowed to offer an improvised performance, although you must then submit details of any stimulus used, eg a chord pattern, melodic ideas (perhaps based on notes of a particular rãg), or text for a song, as well as detailed information about your working methods.

If your specialism happens to be music technology, you can offer a sequenced piece. If this is your choice, then you must use a minimum of *three simultaneously sounding parts*.

At some point during the course your solo performance will be recorded, marked by your teacher and then sent off to an external examiner who will check your teacher's marking. As well as the recording, they'll need a copy of the score.

This is slightly more involved in that you have to offer *two* pieces, one of which **must** be Composition 1. One of the two must be an ensemble item – either Composition 1 or the other work you offer. You could therefore present either:

(a) Composition 1 (solo piece) and an ensemble piece

or

(b) Composition 1 (ensemble piece) and either a solo or an ensemble piece.

Any instrument is allowed and again there is total freedom as to the style of your music. For your ensemble work, performances in class, school music groups or out-of-school groups (eg a rock band) are all encouraged. However it is essential that your final performances are in the presence of your GCSE music teacher who will mark them. One of the performances must be recorded and sent with a copy of the score to the moderators.

If you choose to include a solo piece in your Performing During the Course, it can be any of the following:

Your teacher will be responsible for meeting Edexcel's deadlines, but you should aim to complete coursework by the end of the spring term.

Any instrument is allowed, including the voice, or you can present a performance using music technology. So when we refer to 'instrument' in this chapter we include singing and performance produced through the use of ICT.

Solo Performing

Performing During the Course

For more on Composition 1, see page 24.

The definition of ensemble is a group of two or more players

- a piece on the same instrument that you used for solo performing

- a piece on a different instrument

- solo performing using a sequencer (you must use a minimum of three different simultaneously-sounding voices).

For your ensemble performance(s) you can choose any of the following:

- performing in an ensemble. Note your part must not be doubled (ie played or sung by other people as well as yourself). This means that you cannot choose to sing soprano in a choir with lots of other sopranos, or to play cello in an orchestra with other cellists

- directing an ensemble

- improvising in an ensemble

- performing an ensemble piece using music technology.

If you offer music technology, note that:

- sequences must contain at least three different simultaneously-sounding voices

- mix-downs of multi-track recordings must be of at least three tracks; they may include other performers if you wish, and they can include sequences and/or sampled sounds.

One of these two pieces will, of course, be **Composition 1**. For this you must provide a score, although it does not have to be in conventional notation. However it will have to be detailed enough so that your teacher (and an examiner) can judge how well you are peforming the music.

Remember that it is your performance of the music that is being assessed here, not the composition itself.

You will need to supply a recording of your Solo Performance and a copy of the score. Your teacher will provide details on a Record Sheet provided by Edexcel. You will also need to supply a recording of **one** of the two Performing During the Course pieces and a copy of the score for that piece. However when your teacher completes the Record Sheet they will need to give details of **both** pieces.

What standard should the music be?

The teacher marking your performance will decide on one of three levels that best describes the difficulty of the music that you perform – Easier, Standard or More Difficult. Although you will score the best marks for a more difficult piece played well, you should remember that if you play a piece that is too difficult for you and have to keep stopping, you are likely to score fewer marks than you would have for an easier piece played accurately. Remember, you will probably be a little nervous anyway in front of a micro-phone, so you need to be confident with your chosen piece. Marks will be awarded for accuracy and also for style, both of which will be improved by choosing music that you play with confidence.

Solo Performing

For your solo performance, the key advice is to perform music that you can play well, even accounting for nerves in an examination. You will not do yourself any favours by attempting a piece that is beyond you in terms of difficulty.

Concentrate on preparing to deliver a *musical* performance. This requires paying attention to many factors, including dynamics, intonation, rhythm and tempo, phrasing, and communicating the mood and character of your piece to the listener. For example if you are playing a lively dance piece, good tempo and rhythmic vitality are essential for an uplifting performance. Conversely, a sad and reflective piece can be ruined by an inappropriate choice of tempo and dynamics.

When you select your piece, consult with your teacher to find one that demonstrates your abilities to good effect and is appropriate for your particular instrument. Remember that some types of music, such as technical studies, may not have enough variety in dynamics or note patterns for you to show a range of skills as a performer. Also be a little wary of arrangements: a piece of music originally written for a violin might not work so well on the trumpet. A piece that you know very well and that you have played for ages might not be a good idea as you might offer up a worn out, casual rendition.

If your piece has an accompaniment, make sure that you find someone to play it and that you rehearse with them. Do not leave this until the day before your examination, as you might find it difficult to produce the sort of performance you hoped for. Several rehearsals will not only give you confidence, but will help make the accompanist's job easier too.

As a preparation for your examination, try to play your piece to others, be it in class, to your parents, friends, relations – whoever! This will be extremely useful in building up your confidence in performing in front of an audience. In addition try to rehearse in the actual venue that you will be playing in. It is far better to know how you will sound in advance and you will have the opportunity to experiment with different dynamics, to choose the best place to stand or sit when performing, and to make sure you and your accompanist (if you're using one) can see each other.

Before you perform, ensure that your instrument is warmed up (piano excepted, although warming-up exercises such as scales and arpeggios are a good idea). Also make sure that your instrument is in tune with the piano.

Ensemble performance/direction

Of course many of the comments and hints for solo performance are equally applicable to ensemble performance. However when you play with others, there are some additional factors to consider.

Remember that it is you who is being examined even though this

---

For solo performance, you will be marked in the following way:

1. Accuracy (10 marks)
2. Interpretation (15 marks).

'Accuracy' means making as few mistakes as possible and being able to play in tune. If there are frequent hesitations you will not get a good mark for accuracy. 'Interpretation' is about how musical your playing is and the way that you interpret the music in terms of style. Make sure you pay attention to articulation, phrasing, dynamics and so on.

For ensemble performance, you will be marked in the following way:

1. Accuracy (10 marks)
2. Interpretation (15 marks).

'Accuracy' means making as few mistakes as possible and being able to play in tune. Make sure the instruments are all in tune with one another. 'Interpretation' means delivering a stylish performance, and showing an awareness of balance and integration with the other players. Remember that you are not a soloist here.

part of the Performance paper requires you to play in an ensemble, or to direct one or to present one using music technology. If you cannot be heard then your teacher and examiner cannot very easily mark you, so make sure that your part in the ensemble is not doubled by another instrument. You will also need to be aware of the other performers' abilities when choosing your music as a bad performance from them will definitely let you down. Talk to your teacher and get advice if you are at all unsure.

If you are directing an ensemble, the musical outcome of each rehearsal and the direction that you give the performers are of utmost importance.

It can be difficult to arrange adequate rehearsals. It is easier if all the players come from your GCSE music group and you can rehearse in lesson time. Even so, members of the group may miss vital rehearsals because of illness or other commitments – or they may forget to bring their instruments or music. It is therefore essential to plan well ahead and allow many more weeks than you assume will be needed for ensemble work. You will also need to be firm in establishing the principle that a rehearsal is not a practice. Members of the group need to practise their music before coming to the rehearsal, so that the time you spend together can be used productively to achieve real skill in ensemble performance.

Improvising as part of an ensemble

The key elements in any good improvisation are that your performance is fluent and that it makes musical sense. In addition you need to demonstrate an ability to extend and develop your original ideas. All of this takes practice, so start off by working to a simple chord structure, such as the 12-bar blues. This is fully explained in Area of Study 3, Popular Song in Context.

In the early stages, practise improvising over this chord pattern. A good idea would be to record your ensemble simply playing through the chord pattern and then to use this on your own to practise building up a fluent melody line.

When you feel confident at this exercise, join up with a friend and try some duo improvising. A good way to develop this would be to try to create a musical dialogue between you and the other performer. The stimulus for your improvisation could be a simple melodic outline, a rhythm or a chord pattern. Record your improvising so that you can play it back and appraise the performance. Was it fluent? Did it make musical sense? Was the development of ideas coherent?

You might wish to try to improvise as part of a larger ensemble, such as a jazz group. Decide on the stimulus and plan the structure of your improvisation clearly. It is worth keeping notes of the decisions you make as the rehearsals progress. Ensure that you feature at least one instrumental break to demonstrate the potential of the instrument and your ability as performer.

Don't forget that your ensemble skills are being assessed as well as the quality of the improvisation.

For improvising in an ensemble, you will be marked in the following way:

1. Improvising quality (10 marks)
2. Ensemble skill (15 marks).

Your playing must be fluent and imaginative. You must improvise effectively as part of an ensemble, and show sensitivity to and awareness of what other members of your ensemble are doing.

A convincing performance will demonstrate:
1. a good sense of style
2. detailed attention to articulation and phrasing
3. good range of dynamic contrast
4. secure intonation.

You should remember that your part must blend and balance with the ensemble, and that you need to react and show awareness of the other performers in the group. To achieve this, you need to listen carefully to the overall sound: take recordings and use them to improve your performance.

Performance using music technology

In this option you are able to submit mix-downs of multi-track recordings. You must feature at least three tracks. The tracks can be recorded using microphones, sampled or sequenced or by using a combination of these methods. The end result must be a stereo mix. Remember that in this option you are assessed not only for the performance but also for the post-production work and the final mixing down. You must make sure that you give each of these areas due attention.

You will be assessed on how accurate and fluent the piece is. So take care when recording each track to ensure the parts are accurate. In the case of multi-tracking, you will need to make sure that samples match in terms of tempi and complement each other well. Other ensemble skills that will be assessed include the use of stereo field, balance, equalisation and effects in the finished recording. You will also be assessed on your sense of style. As you build up your piece, get into the habit of playing tracks back. Ask yourself if the style is consistent throughout. What you should be aiming for at the end of the process is a clear, focused recording.

You can include this option as your Composition 1 performance. Your part may be performed live or sequenced and you may include other performers. However if you take this option, you will also have to provide a score or a copy of the recording(s) that provided the stimulus for your work, so that the moderator can assess your part in the overall performance.

For performing using music technology, you will be marked in the following way:
1. Accuracy (10 marks)
2. Ensemble skill (15 marks).

'Accuracy' means that as few mistakes as possible occur, especially in pitch and rhythm. Sequencing must have well-shaped dynamics, appropriate use of modulation, pitch bend, attack, phrasing and effective timbre choices. Recording must demonstrate a good use of equalisation (EQ) and effects, and dynamic range. Tracks should be in time and should complement each other well. In general a good sense of style and overall balance is required.

Composing

Composition is not an isolated activity: it should arise from your experiences in performing and listening. You might well have enjoyed performing, for example, a set of variations on your instrument and you would like to use these as a model for your own composition. Likewise, you might have recently studied the 12-bar blues and now want to write your own blues composition. This is *exactly what your teacher wants.* They would like you to come up with some ideas, because if you are motivated enough to want to compose something that you have chosen yourself, then the chances are that you will do well.

The link with Listening and Performing is important. Once you have decided what you want to do, try to listen and perform as much music in that style or form as possible. If you are going to write a 12-bar blues, listen to different types of the form, such as an early blues song, a modern blues song, some early instrumental blues, and some modern instrumental blues. In other words, immerse yourself in the music and play some too, if you are able. This will give you a good grounding and knowledge of different styles before you start. Try to choose a format that will let you experiment with different textures and techniques. One of the common criticisms of student compositions is their lack of textural variety. All instrumental or vocal parts playing or singing for all of the time is likely to be dull.

What you have to do

You will be expected to produce **two** compositions (or arrangements) lasting at least **three minutes in total**.

It is possible to offer the following combinations:

(a) two compositions, *or*

(b) two arrangements, *or*

(c) one composition **and** one arrangement.

Both of your pieces will need to be written to a set brief based on topics in *two different* Areas of Study, for example, a set of variations (Area of Study 1) *and* a minimalist composition (Area of Study 2).

Composition 1 **must** be performed as one of two Performing During the Course pieces.

What to write for

If you write an ensemble piece it would be sensible to write for instruments/voices available in your music class to make it easier to rehearse your work in lesson time. Or if you perform in an ensemble – such as a pop group, jazz band, flute group, choir, orchestra, string quartet or brass band – why not write a piece for that group? You are given free rein to write for whatever you wish. Compositions could be for voices, acoustic instruments or electronic instruments. Other types of music technology can also be used, eg sequencing, mixing and so on. As two of the possible topics relate

Your teacher will be responsible for meeting Edexcel's deadlines, but you should aim to complete coursework by the end of the spring term.

Beware: group compositions are not allowed. The pieces must be composed or arranged by you alone.

to these procedures, namely electronic music and club dance remix, then you could use one of these types of music as a basis for your own compositions. However note that neither the actual recording nor scores printed with the aid of music technology will be assessed.

A word of warning. The moderators are fully aware of the various songwriting and sequencing programmes available these days, such as *Dance eJay*, and will be able to spot abuse of these programmes. Any composition that shows little or no original work will receive very few marks.

Arrangements

These are perfectly acceptable instead of free compositions. You may arrange any piece of music for whatever combination you wish eg *Greensleeves* for sitar, flute and djembe. What is more important is the music itself. The following illustrates **good** (high marks) and **bad** (low marks) approaches.

You take *Greensleeves* and create a new version of the piece with significant changes to the original, for example different instrumentation, new harmony, a different type of accompaniment, varied textures, different key, changes to the rhythm and tempo, a new structure and so on. If this is done effectively and musically you deserve a high mark. **A good approach**

You take *Greensleeves* and simply transcribe it for instruments of your choice. You don't make any significant changes to the structure, texture, etc. You deserve a low mark. **A poor approach**

You must enclose the original stimulus in your coursework submission so that the moderator can assess the extent of effective change in your arrangement.

The brief

Each of the two briefs must be based on a topic from different Areas of Study. You can devise your own briefs or they may be set by your teacher. It would make good sense to discuss with your teacher the ideas that will most excite and stimulate you. Remember that you will be working on the compositions for some time, so make sure that the briefs suit your aims and interests. The brief must describe the nature of the composition, how it relates to a topic in an Area of Study, and should also give the moderators a clear idea of your intentions. You must refer to some or all of the following: purpose, resources, effect, time and place. For example:

◆ the brief might be to compose a piece in ternary form (Area of Study 1)

◆ the purpose might be to write it for a school play

◆ the resources might be a brass group or other existing ensemble

◆ the desired effect might be to create music to cover a scene change

◆ the time and place might be Victorian England.

Edexcel will provide you with forms called 'Understanding the Brief' which you should submit for each composition.

You will be asked to complete the following questions:

◆ What was your composition (or arrangement) brief?

◆ How does your composition (or arrangement) meet the brief?

◆ What improvements did you make to your work when you were composing or arranging the music? This could include any adjustments you made after performances of it.

You should make connections with performance (you have to perform Composition 1) and with the relevant Area of Study. For example if you have written a piece of minimalist music, relate the processes that you have used (such as phasing, ostinatos, note addition/subtraction etc) to works that you have studied by minimalist composers, such as Terry Riley and Steve Reich.

As it is easy to forget what you did, when you did it and in what order, make sure you keep an ongoing log of the compositional processes from initial ideas to the last double barline. This can be done easily during the course and you can then simply summarise your notes at the end.

Submission requirements

For each piece, you *must* provide the following three items:

1. a notated score (hand-written or printed) **or** a written commentary

2. a recording (cassette, CD or minidisc) – note that the quality of recorded performances is **not** assessed

3. the completed 'Understanding the brief' document.

Your composition

Planning

Planning is very important. If you are writing for an ensemble, it is vital to write for people who will be around for the entire time that you are writing the piece. That probably means people either in your class or in an ensemble in which you regularly perform.

A good starting point is to find out about the instruments and performers that you will be writing for. You will need to know the range of each instrument, what constitutes good idiomatic writing for the instruments and the technical abilities of each player. You will also need to think about breathing for singers and wind players, bowing for string players, pedalling for pianists and so on. Remember that music technology is not much help in some of these practical matters. For instance even if your synthesiser can produce a sound like a trumpet, it probably will not warn you that you have written notes that are out of the range of a human player or that you have demanded the impossible and asked a single trumpeter to play a chord. It certainly will not remind you that your trumpet part has continued for several minutes without a single breathing point. Nor will it tell you how long a rest you need for the player to fit a mute or turn a page. So planning is also about finding out. It might be a good idea to keep notes on your findings.

This will help when you come to fill in the 'Understanding the brief' form at the end of the process.

Group improvising is always a good way in which to find out about the sounds and capabilities of different instruments. Of course these ideas can later be incorporated into your own composition. Much of it you may well reject, but equally you might discover an idea with potential for development, so jot it down. When you have written a tune for your instrument, try it out several times. Does it work or does a part of it need changing?

In all of your planning, try to listen to and play as much music as possible, not only for the ensemble itself, but also in the style or form that you intend to incorporate in your own piece.

Theory

You will feel much more confident about composing if you have a good grasp of the fundamentals such as notation, chords, keys and cadences. After studying pages 7–18 of this book you could work through publications like the Associated Board theory books. This can be done at your own pace and your teacher or instrumental tutor should be able to help you. As a rough guide, if you can work up to about grade 5 theory by the end of your course, you will have a good grasp of most of the common musical techniques and devices. Having said that, a lot of useful harmony is featured in the Grade 6 Theory Workbook, plus an excellent in-depth study of how melodies are constructed and developed in a variety of styles.

Getting started

Where do you get your ideas for a composition in the first place? Do you start with a motif, a tune, a rhythm, a chord pattern or a form? A good way of discovering your opening idea is by improvising, singing, or even whistling. Inspiration can come in many forms. It could be a particularly interesting chord pattern on the piano or a riff on the bass guitar. The key thing is to write an idea down as soon as it occurs to you.

Development

As a simple rule, assess your musical idea in terms of its potential for growth. A good idea will have something characteristic about it, maybe a rhythmic feature such as a triplet figuration or a melodic interval such as a leap of a minor 7th. These ideas can then be used when you develop the opening melody. Beginning is sometimes the easiest bit. You write down the opening stimulus (tune, chords or rhythm) and the most common problem is what to do next. Here are some suggestions designed to help.

Many people fall into the trap of simply repeating their opening idea (which might well be promising) until they (and everyone else) are sick of it. The result of this approach leads to a sense of too little variety and no contrasts. The piece goes nowhere and appears static and dull. Another problem is an opening that is followed by a multitude of new ideas, one after the other, so that the piece lacks direction and cohesion.

You need *some* repetition and *some* development of ideas. A good compromise can be struck by using different types of repetition – there are many examples of such techniques in the works you will study for your Listening exam. If you pay particular attention to these you will learn a good deal about how to keep your audience fascinated by material which seems both new and yet strangely familiar. This is the way that most composers have learnt their craft for centuries: first studying and borrowing elements from existing works in order to learn the basics of composing, and then developing their own approaches in order to communicate something new.

In particular study what happens in pieces that you perform. Understanding how they are constructed will not only give you ideas for your own composition but will also give you a much better insight into how you might plan your own performances in order to bring out structural details. Music needs contrasting points of conflict, climax and repose. Planning these will help you to produce much more effective compositions – and performances.

Your teacher will help you to analyse how one of your favourite pieces has been composed. There is no harm whatsoever in using a piece as a model for composition, as long as you don't copy it too slavishly. That's called plagiarism or cheating.

Composing takes considerable time and you must be prepared to revise and rework your initial ideas. That's why it is best to start on your compositions as early in the course as possible.

Simple techniques

Let's assume that you have composed a short musical idea: how might this be extended? There are three basic ways to approach this task.

Repetition   The repetition could be exact, or an ascending or descending **sequence**. It is quite effective to repeat your idea one tone higher (or lower), as it will sound as if the music is developing naturally.

Invention   You can also try to invent a contrasting melody to the opening idea. Then you will have two ideas that can be developed separately or together in the rest of your piece.

Variation   A varied version of your opening idea can also be quite effective and will sound as if the opening melody is developing.

These methods are useful ways of extending your composition. Experiment with each and see which seems to work best for your particular piece. Also look at other similar compositions. What techniques were used in that piece?

If you are adopting a conventional musical style (such as an imitation of Mozart or of classic rock and roll) try to write your music in balanced phrases. Usually a phrase will last for two, four or eight bars, and this is answered and balanced by another phrase of the same length.

If you keep this idea in mind as you compose, then you should end up with some well-structured music.

But if you feel confident, a structure that is not always based on balanced phrases may sound more enterprising and less predictable. For instance it is often possible to create an effective three-bar phrase with an overlap – in which the last bar of one phrase becomes the first bar of the next.

Even if you decide to write in mainly four-bar balanced phrases, your piece will be much more interesting if the last note of the phrase (often a semibreve) is enlivened by some interest in another part, such as a lively and syncopated one-bar link motif. This will give something of interest for your performers, especially if it is assigned to a middle part or bass part that has not so far been very interesting. Go and take a look at *GAM* page 108, bars 15–16, 20, 23–24.

Structure

Binary and ternary forms

From the outset you should think about the overall plan. If you are writing a 12-bar blues or a composition on a ground bass, then you will already have a strong structure. Likewise if you are going to write a song the lyrics and the verse-chorus format will help you to write a balanced and logical structure. However you could consider two of the simplest and most effective structures: binary and ternary forms.

Ternary form is discussed in more detail in pages 35–38.

◆ binary: two sections AB (each usually repeated)

◆ ternary: three-part form ABA.

In the B section in both forms, your music may well benefit from a reasonable contrast to the first section. One of the fundamental contrasts is that of key. In ternary form for example, section B is often in the dominant (or another related key). Here are several ways in which you could achieve contrast in your ternary composition. Don't forget these aren't rules for how ternary form works. They are only suggestions for you to act on if you wish. Don't attempt to use them all or you may end up with too much contrast.

In what follows capital letters are used to show how music is structured. (This is a standard system and you will come across it in lots of books.) For instance, AB indicates that a first section (A) is followed by a different section (B). If the first section is restated at the end the form would be described as ABA. Numbers are attached to the letters to indicate that significant variation has occurred. So A–A^1–A^2 indicates that the first section (A) is repeated with two different variations.

Method of contrast	Section A	Section B
Key	tonic	dominant
Or	major	relative minor
Character	rhythmic and lively	lyrical and sustained
Tempo	fast	slow
Dynamics	loud	soft
Articulation	legato	staccato
Texture	full sound	thinner sound

Variations

Another popular form is theme and variations and this will give you a firm structure to follow. It is a form that enables you to work in small chunks, one variation at a time.

After you have written out the theme, which could be your own

Variations are discussed in more detail in pages 43–47.

original creation or a borrowed theme, you need to think of ways of varying it. Some useful procedures are:

◆ varying the note values (if the theme is in crotchets, try adding quavers, triplets or dotted notes in the variations)

◆ changing mode from major to minor or vice versa

◆ writing a syncopated version

◆ changing the harmony (if you have used chords) or keeping the same harmony but adding a new tune

◆ composing a rapid semiquaver toccata-like variation

◆ changing the metre, eg from duple to triple time

◆ introducing imitation between parts.

Try listening to a number of sets of variations in order to get some ideas for your own piece. For example the 12 Mozart piano variations on *Ah, vous dirai-je, maman?* (otherwise known as *Twinkle, twinkle little star.*) These contain some interesting ideas that you could use in your own variations. Turn to page 35, where this song is discussed.

Rondo

Rondo forms are discussed in more detail in pages 47–51.

A rondo is a form such as ABACA where A is the rondo theme that keeps coming round, while B and C are contrasting episodes. This form features both **repetition** and **contrast**.

Episodes B and C need to be significantly different from the A section. Contrasts could include being in a different key to the refrain, such as the dominant, subdominant, relative minor or major.

Again, listen to some examples (such as those in *GAM*). There are many available – you might even have played one yourself in the past. Dig it out and play it through again now to see how the music is constructed. Write on the music itself how the episodes are different from the main rondo theme. If you wish, use the structure as a model for your own rondo composition.

Song writing

Many of you may opt for using words as the structure for your music. A pattern of alternating verses and choruses can provide a strong basic structure for your piece.

A song can be a piece for unaccompanied solo voice or unaccompanied voices singing in parts. But you might prefer to write an accompaniment, perhaps for piano or guitar or for a group of instruments (such as a chamber ensemble or rhythm section), or a sequenced and synthesised backing track. Whichever you go for, make sure that all the parts, not just the main vocal line, have melodic and/or rhythmic interest of their own.

Rhythm

When setting a text to music, remember that both music and poetry have rhythm. Your first job is to decide where the natural accents occur in the poem. The easiest way to do this is to speak the words aloud, underlining the syllables that attract a natural stress, eg:

'A<u>bout</u>, a<u>bout</u>, in <u>reel</u> and <u>rout</u>
The <u>death</u>-fires <u>danced</u> at <u>night</u>;
The <u>water</u>, <u>like</u> a <u>witch</u>'s <u>oils</u>,
Burnt <u>green</u>, and <u>blue</u> and <u>white</u>.

('The Rime of the Ancient Mariner' by Coleridge)

The underlined syllables should fall on strong beats. In this example you would have to begin with an upbeat (see *right*).

A - bout, a - bout, in reel and rout The death

This process is called working out the scansion of the poem. If your music follows the rhythm of the poem too predictably, you risk boring your audience: sometimes shifting the stress on to a surprising syllable can create just the dramatic effect you need. Above all, a poem's scansion does not force you into using any one particular metre. Choose your underlying rhythmic pattern, but look for places to break that pattern. If you find your melody is developing around repeated notes or too much stepwise movement try looking for some dramatic places to use a leap. It can be a good way of drawing out the importance of a particular word if the melody jumps to a high note.

Singers will be grateful if high notes are set to an open vowel sound that is easy to sing such as 'ah', although this is not always possible with English-language texts. Remember that singers need places in which to breath: these can be good opportunities for the accompaniment to emerge with a short motif of its own.

If you write an accompanied song, don't double the vocal-part with the accompaniment throughout as it can sound very dull – although short sections in which the piano doubles the voice in a different octave can provide a welcome change of texture. Whatever type of setting you choose, try to ensure that all of the parts have interest of their own – if the lower voices merely copy the rhythms of the melody, or the piano part consists of endless minims and semibreves, your work is unlikely to score high marks.

Underlay

The way that syllables are written underneath notes is called **underlay**. Many candidates (and some computer programs) seem to have trouble getting this right but the basic principles are quite simple and well worth learning.

✦ Spaced hyphens are used to split long words into their separate syllables, eg ho - li - day.

✦ Split words between consonants whenever possible: eg mag - net, dis - mal. If there is only one central consonant, split the word before that consonant, eg o - pen, de - mon.

✦ When there are no central consonants hyphenate between the vowels: eg cha - os, flu - id. But never split diphthongs (compound vowels that are pronounced together): eg 'point' should always be written as a single word and never hyphenated as 'po - int'.

✦ Take care over syllables that are frequently run together in ordinary speech – for example you may need to decide whether you want his-to-ry or his't'ry, or if you prefer gov-ern-ment to gov'-ment. Notice how an apostrophe is used if you want to show an elision in an English word.

- Don't split up single syllables with hyphens.

- An extension line is used when a monosyllabic word or the last syllable of a polysyllabic word is extended by a tied note or by additional notes sung to the same syllable, eg love._____

- Put any punctuation before extension lines.

- Write slurs over notes that are sung to the same syllable.

Make sure that you have a good contrast between the tune of the verse and the tune of the chorus. It is usually the chorus that we recall most readily when we think of a song, so try to write a catchy melody that can be easily remembered.

In addition, you could write a short instrumental **introduction** and a **coda** at the end. Many songs also have instrumental sections to break up the strict verse-chorus-verse-chorus structure. These are called 'interludes', or in pop and jazz 'instrumental breaks'. Try to write one break just before the final verse to create an impact.

Melodic writing

While the creation of the melody is something for you to decide upon, it is worth highlighting several important elements of a melody that you might consider.

- The shape or contour. This is the way the notes rise and fall during the phrase. A good melody should have shape and direction. Make sure that your melody has points of climax (often high notes) and repose (often notes of a lower pitch).

- The range of the melody. Does your melody need only a small range of notes, or is it dramatic, needing a wide range for expression?

- The key of your melody. Is it major, minor or modal?

- Melodies should usually contain a mixture of steps and leaps. Don't be afraid of repeating notes; these can be very effective. For example the British national anthem contains repeated notes and step-wise movements. Simple, yet effective.

- Remember that many famous melodies are formed from two basic building blocks: notes of triads (often the tonic triad) and notes of the scale.

- Melodies don't have to consist entirely of notes: rests can be just as effective.

Many famous melodies have survived because they are easy to remember, sing or hum. Think about a few of the melodies that you know well – you will be surprised at how simple and repetitive many of them are.

Writing accompaniments

No matter how good your melodic writing is, it is worth learning to write some form of accompaniment. You'll find that you need a knowledge of basic harmony for this: check your understanding of chords in the 'Understanding Music' section if you are unsure.

Very few pieces other than hymn tunes have four block-chords in every bar. Study pieces that you like and note how often the harmony changes (this is called the rate of harmonic change). In some pieces there may be only one chord per bar, or the same chord may even be used throughout several bars.

Try to develop your basic chords into interesting patterns so that the accompaniment flows and has a life of its own. Look at several pieces of music to discover the types of accompaniment used, such as broken chords, flowing quavers or repeated notes. Notice how counter-melodies can add variety and how the accompaniment can provide a little melodic interest at the ends of phrases in order to give your soloist a rest and to take the music forward into the next phrase. Remember too that the accompaniment does not have to be continuous: use rests and changes in texture to enrich your music.

See Figuration on page 16.

In addition to chords, there are some simple types of accompaniments to consider.

✦ A drone is commonly found in folk music, where a continuous note or notes accompany the melody. Often two notes a 5th apart are used. They are invariably the tonic and dominant. In C major, these would be C and G.

✦ An ostinato is a repeated pattern. The pattern itself could be a rhythm, a tune, a chord pattern or all three.

Beginnings and endings

How you start and end a piece is very important, as we tend to remember the first thing that we hear and the last. When writing stories, we are often told to make sure that our story has a good beginning and end. Much the same applies to composing.

To begin you could have:

✦ an accompaniment pattern – then bring the tune in after several bars

✦ a special introductory passage such as a fanfare

✦ one part after the other building up the texture – a gradual start

✦ a sudden, dramatic start.

To end you could have:

✦ a gradual fade out

✦ a closing section, called a coda

✦ a slow down of the tempo, perhaps with the use of longer notes

✦ a sudden, dramatic stop.

Exploiting your resources

Your composition may be going very well, but just stop and ask yourself who has the tune and for how long have they had it to themselves. If the answer is (i) the top part and (ii) all the time, then the risk is that the other parts are probably dull.

Even if you are only writing for two instruments, say flute and piano, give the piano some melodic interest for at least part of the time.

If you are writing for a small ensemble, for example a woodwind quintet, try to break your melody into fragments and pass them around the instruments. This will create some interesting and varied textures.

Do not be afraid of rests. It is not compulsory to fill every bar with notes. If you use rests effectively, then not only will you add some lightness to your music, but the ear will be relieved of the tiring sound of a thick, full texture with all the parts playing away continuously.

Refining the end product

One of the best ways to improve your composition is to rehearse it and then change the parts that did not work well. Let your performers have their say. They will quickly be able to point out unplayable bits and you can then rewrite as necessary. Rehearsal will also help you to hear the whole sound of the music together. Ask yourself the following questions:

◆ Does it have the intended effect?

◆ Is the balance wrong in places, so that the tune is not heard clearly?

◆ Are some of your harmonies wrong?

◆ Does the structure hold together convincingly?

Your teacher is there to assist with advice, so don't be afraid to ask.

Don't simply play through the composition several times at each rehearsal. Concentrate on the sections that you have rewritten. Do they work now, or do you need to adjust them further? This chiselling away at your music is constructive, because you are refining your work as you go along. Eventually you must, like an artist, put down your brushes and stand back. If you are pleased with your work, then stop.

Repetition and contrast in western classical music 1600–1899

Ternary form

Ternary form consists of three sections in the pattern ABA:

Example 1 Anonymous *Twinkle, twinkle little star*

Example 1 shows an important feature of many ternary-form pieces. The two phrases marked A form closed units – sections which, because they end on the tonic, sound complete in themselves. But phrase B has an open ending that finishes on the supertonic and so prepares the way for the repeat of phrase A.

The B section clearly differs from the A section, but can you spot why it sounds like part of the same piece? Not only is its rhythm the same, but also its tune is a sequence of the last four bars of section A (which is then repeated to complete the B section).

Such simplicity and repetition are among the things that make nursery rhymes memorable, but other types of music are usually more complicated. For instance, to provide an even number of phrases, the first section might be repeated (AABA) – this is still ternary form, though. Or the A section might be varied when it returns. We could show this as ABA[1]. Try writing your own varied repeat of the A section, perhaps something like this:

For more ideas on varying this melody see Mozart's 12 variations for piano on *Ah, vous dirai-je Maman* (a French tune that is the same as *Twinkle, twinkle little star*). This work will also help your study of variations – a topic we will explore later in this chapter.

Later we shall see that in longer ternary-form compositions, A and B can be substantial sections rather than just short phrases.

Many 19th-century character pieces are in ternary form. Some of them aim to express one or two specific emotions. Ternary form is ideal when the composer wants to express two moods because they can be expressed through the contrasting music of sections A and B, while the return of section A ensures musical coherence. Example 2 is the melody from a character piece for piano by Schumann (1810–1856). It comes from a collection of children's pieces (*Album for the Young*) that he composed in 1848.

Character pieces

Example 2   Schumann, melody of 'Little Folk Song' from *Album for the Young*

Rico Gulda's recording of the *Album for the Young* (*Album für die Jugend*) is available on *Naxos 8.555711*.

The A section is closed (it ends with finality on the tonic), while section B is open (it ends inconclusively on the dominant). But in Example 2 there is much more contrast between sections A and B than there is in Example 1, for instance:

◆ the rhythms of A are formed from smoothly flowing crotchets and minims, while the jagged rhythms in section B are formed from shorter note values

◆ the melody of section A includes a lot of conjunct (stepwise) movement, while the melody in section B is mainly triadic – it outlines simple chords such as the D-major and A-major triads at the beginning and end of bar 9

◆ section A is in D minor, while section B is in D major

◆ as a result of the minor–major difference and the much shorter note lengths in B, the moods are highly contrasted – sad in A, cheerful in B.

Despite these contrasting elements the two sections are united by:

◆ both sharing the same tonic (D)

◆ both falling into regular two-bar phrases

◆ both containing grace notes followed by an octave leap to the dominant.

Tchaikovsky, Dance of the Reed Pipes

GAM page 61   CD1 Track 26
The Nutcracker: 'Dance of the Reed Pipes'
Tchaikovsky (1840–1893)

The 'Dance of the Reed Pipes' is one of a set of characteristic dances in Tchaikovsky's ballet *The Nutcracker* (1892). On paper it looks fairly complicated, but when you listen to it you will immediately spot the ternary-form structure brought about by the change from D major to F♯ minor at bar 43, and the return to D major and the original melody at bar 62. So, leaving out the two-bar introduction (which sets the oom-pah accompaniment going), the first statement of section A begins at bar 3 and ends, as expected, with a perfect cadence in the tonic key of D major in bar 42 – a total of 40 bars. Yet the restatement of section A lasts only 16 bars (from bar 62 to the end). How come? Well, if you listen to the first 42 bars again you will notice a new theme played on the cor anglais in bars 19–24. Then, after two bars of chord V (coloured with chromatic notes) bars 3–15 are repeated (bars 27–39) followed by three bars ending with the perfect cadence we have already noticed (bars 41–42). So the first A section is itself a mini-ternary structure:

X (bars 3–18)	Y (bars 19–26)	X (bars 27–42)

Notice that when section A returns after the middle episode Tchaikovsky chooses to repeat bars 27–42 rather than bars 3–18. This is because, as we have seen, there is a perfect cadence in the tonic in bars 41–42 whereas bar 18 ends with chord V moving seamlessly into the cor-anglais melody.

Handel, 'He was despised'

In 18th-century operas and oratorios the most common type of solo song was a type of ternary form called the **da capo aria**. It was given this name because the Italian phrase *da capo al fine* or the abbreviation 'D.C.' was written at the end of the music to indicate that the first section of the aria should be repeated, the end of the repeat being marked with the word *fine*. 'He was despised' from Handel's *Messiah* (1742) is a da capo aria. Section A (bars 1–49) contrasts strongly with section B (bars 50–67). Notice that section A ends with the expected perfect cadence in the tonic key of E♭ major, whereas section B begins in C minor and ends with a perfect cadence in G minor.

In the da capo aria it was common for the soloist to improvise ornamentation when the A section was repeated. If you compare different recordings of the aria you will notice different approaches to embellishment. Section A and therefore the whole aria is framed by almost identical orchestral passages. These are called **ritornelli** and you will notice that parts of them appear between the vocal phrases (eg bars 21–24). Remember these ritornelli – we will encounter them again in the baroque concerto.

Mozart, Symphony No. 40: movement III

In early 18th-century suites two dances of the same type were often paired together. It was standard practice to repeat the first of them after the second, so forming a simple ternary structure (ABA). The only baroque dance to survive in late 18th-century classical instrumental music was the **minuet**. This was paired with another minuet which, because the texture was sometimes reduced to three parts, became known as a **trio**. In the third movement of Mozart's Symphony No. 40 (1788) the *Menuetto* is scored for full or almost full orchestra up to bar 36, but the clarinets are omitted from the trio and the texture is generally much thinner. The **tutti** scoring of the *Menuetto* contrasts with the more intimate scoring of the trio, but the most obvious contrast is brought about by the simple change from G minor (the tonic key of the minuet) to G major (the tonic key of the trio).

The instruction *D.C. Menuetto* under bars 83–84 means that the minuet should be repeated (but the repeat signs in bars 14 and 42 are usually disregarded in the second performance of the minuet). The direction *Fine* in bar 42 means that the repeat of the minuet

Da capo aria

Da capo al fine means 'from the beginning to the word *fine*' (*fine* means 'end').

GAM page 52   CD1 Track 24
Messiah: 'He was despised'
Handel (1685–1759)

The Tavener Choir's recording of *Messiah* is available on *Veritas VBD 5620042*

Ritornello is Italian for 'little return'. Ritornelli is the plural.

Minuet and trio

GAM page 56   CD1 Track 25
Symphony No. 40: movement III
Mozart (1756–1791)

Not all the instruments play at printed pitch:
◆ clarinets in B♭ sound a tone lower
◆ horns in G sound a perfect 4th lower
◆ the double-basses sound an octave lower. They play in octaves with the cellos throughout the movement.

and the entire movement should end at this point. The overall ternary structure is shown *below*.

A	B	A
(minuet in G minor)	(trio in G major)	(minuet in G minor)

Test yourself on ternary form

1. In the 'Dance of the Reed Pipes' how does the texture of bars 43–50 differ from the texture of bars 62–70?

   ....

   ....

2. How does Handel achieve a complete change of mood between the two sections of 'He was despised'?

   ....

   ....

3. Compare the key structure of the Minuet and Trio from Mozart's Symphony No. 40 with Example 2. Do you notice any similarities?

   ....

   ....

Performing

If you can't find a ternary-form piece, try either of the following Welsh tunes, both of which can be found in many school song, hymn and carol books: Ar Hyd Y Nos ('All Through the Night'), Nos Galan ('Deck the Hall with Boughs of Holly').

Find a short piece in ternary form that you can play or sing. Perform it to the rest of the group and see if your fellow students can spot the return of the first section. Then perform it again and ask them to identify the sections precisely using letters and numbers (for example ABA, AABA, ABA[1], AABA[1], etc). Finally, perform it for a third time and ask the rest of the group to name the ways in which the B section differs from the A sections.

Composing

If inspiration fails you can extend your melody by using sequences.

Write a short ternary-form melody (no more than 16 bars) in which the A section is closed and the B section is open. When you repeat section A you might like to vary it by taking some of its phrases down an octave, by subtly altering the pitch of one or two notes, or by adding a countermelody (as in bars 15–16 of Example 2).

Ground bass

A ground bass is also called simply 'a ground' and in Italian a 'basso ostinato'.

A ground bass is a repeating bass melody above which the composer writes varying melodies and harmonies. A movement using this technique is therefore a continuous set of variations. Indeed instrumental movements built on a ground bass are often entitled 'Variations upon a Ground'. Compositions of this type were common throughout the baroque era (c.1600–1750). They can be found in many types of vocal and instrumental music of the period.

A Grounde (in G minor) by William Byrd (1543–1623) was composed at the beginning of our period. It is a set of variations for the virginal (a small harpsichord) intended for performance in the home. This ground is four bars long and uses only three pitches, *left*.

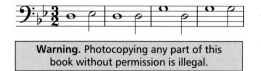

Here are the first two appearances of the ground bass:

Example 3 Byrd, opening bars of *A Grounde*

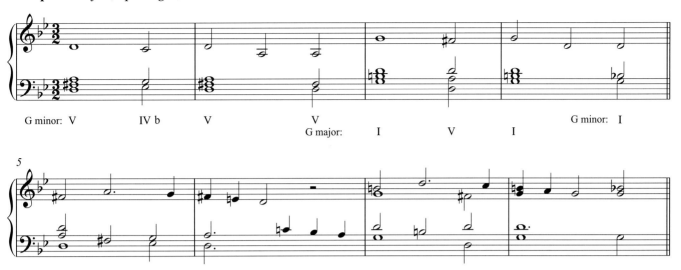

In bars 1–4 you will see that:

♦ the melody is sequential (bars 3–4 are the same as bars 1–2 but at a higher pitch)

♦ Byrd uses only chords I, IVb and V

♦ the music changes from G minor to G major and back again.

The use of melodic sequences, a limited number of chords and slight changes to the basso ostinato are common in baroque ground-bass variations. What these compositions lack in harmonic variety is usually balanced by increasingly complex textures. This is the case in Byrd's *A Grounde* as more and more complex decorations are added until the basso ostinato is almost submerged by flurries of scalic figuration. The first of these variations is shown in bars 5–8. Notice how the bass and the harmony are both essentially the same, but they now support a new melody.

'Dido's Lament' is probably the most famous ground-bass composition ever written. It comes from *Dido and Aeneas* (1689), the only complete opera by Purcell (1659–1695). The ground itself falls in semitones from the tonic (G) to the dominant (D) of G minor, and this is followed by five pitches that suggest a perfect cadence in this key, even when the ground is heard on its own at the start of the air:

Dido and Aeneas

You will find 'Dido's Lament' on pages 356–358 of *NAM*. A recording of the complete opera is available on Harmonia Mundi HMC901683.

Example 4 Purcell, ground from 'When I am laid in earth', *Dido and Aeneas*

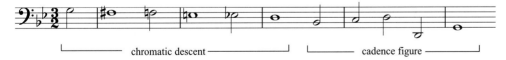

Hundreds of laments composed in the baroque era are based on a bass that descends chromatically from the tonic to the dominant. What distinguishes them is the extent to which the composer achieves both continuity and variety in the melodies and harmonies that are added to the ground, and, in vocal music, the extent to which they express the mood of the words.

Purcell achieves continuity by stating the ground 11 times in succession without any modifications or changes of key.

Look also at the subtle way Dido enters on the last note of the ground (bar 6) and the way her second phrase ('may my wrongs create') begins halfway through the second statement of the ground.

Variety is achieved by the contrast between the long **cantabile** phrases in bars 6–24 and the short phrases in the setting of the words 'Remember me' which reach a climax in bar 33. Look also at the way Purcell radically changes the string orchestra's harmonic progressions. The harmonies become increasingly dissonant. Notice how the melody clashes with the ground: Purcell is vividly expressing Dido's anguish.

Purcell, 'Here the deities approve'

GAM page 9   CD1 Track 1
Welcome to all the pleasures: 'Here the deities approve'
Purcell (1659–1695)

An air is simply a song – the Italian term is aria. An ode is a vocal composition in honour of a person or occasion.

In some performances the first statement of a ground will be completely bare, while in others improvised harmony on one or more continuo instruments might be added.

The first item in *GAM* is 'Here the deities approve'. It is another air on a ground by Purcell. It comes from the ode *Welcome to all the Pleasures*. This ode was intended for performance by a London music society on 22 November 1683, the occasion being the festival of St Cecilia, the patron saint of music. There is repetition but not much contrast in the air in E minor. The ground bass is three bars long – can you spot that there is another chromatic descent (E–D♯–D♮–C♯–C♮–B) woven between other notes in bars 1–2? At the end of bar 3 it finishes on the dominant (B) and thus creates a perfect cadence when the next statement of the ground begins on E in bar 4.

The ground is repeated without change 18 times (each occupies one complete stave). Because it consists of broken chords Purcell is pretty well stuck with the same E-minor harmony.

There are two tunes. The first consists of two phrases, both of them skilfully contrived to cover the cadences of the ground in bars 3–4 and 6–7. It is repeated in bars 9–13. The second tune (bars 14–22) is longer and more complex. Its five phrases reflect the structure of the text. Thus the rhyme of the couplet 'All the talents they have lent you, All the blessings they have sent you' are reflected in an inexact sequence. Purcell would have known full well that a much more exact sequence is possible: the beauty of Purcell is that he almost always avoids the obvious. The perfect cadence at the end of this phrase (bars 15–16) is the first occasion when a vocal cadence coincides with the V–I cadence between the end of one statement of the ground and the beginning of the next. The second phrase ('Pleas'd to see what they bestow') ends with an imperfect cadence which is answered by a perfect cadence at the end of the third phrase (V–I in bars 18–19). The fourth phrase (bars 19^2–20^3) introduces the only chromatic colour in the vocal part (G♯) while the last phrase is a subtle reworking of the third phrase. The whole of the second tune is repeated in bars 23–31.

At the end of bar 30, and overlapping with the soloist's final notes, the upper strings enter to provide a welcome change of texture. Notice how each part has its own melodic interest – this is known as counterpoint. This is particularly easy to see in bar 49, where the second violins enter in imitation of the melody started two beats earlier by the violas (and the first violins imitate the same melody in bar 50).

Apart from these imitative inner parts, the second half of the air is essentially identical to the first half – the first violin plays the singer's melody throughout, but now an octave higher than it was previously. This orchestral ritornello is a harmonised repeat of bars 1–31. In fact in the 58 bars of this aria there are just over 12 bars of melody which Purcell skilfully spins out by repetitions, avoiding monotony by the change of texture from vocal monody to instrumental polyphony.

When you listen to the recording there are three important points to note:

◆ The vocal solo is sung by a countertenor (also known as a male alto). This type of voice is produced by an adult male singer using a vocal technique known as falsetto to produce a range similar to that of a female alto

◆ From bar 10 onwards the singer frequently embellishes the written notes with ornamentation. This was part of the 'performance practice' (the expected technique) in much solo singing and playing of the baroque period

◆ The ground bass is played by a continuo group.

Try to hear a performance of Purcell's most famous ode for St Cecilia's Day, often identified by the first words of the text: 'Hail! bright Cecilia!'.

Basso continuo is a baroque term for a part usually designed for two or more instruments – at least one bass instrument (such as a cello) and one chordal instrument (such as a harpsichord). On this recording you should be able to hear that the chordal instrument is an organ. The player is improvising a 'filling' between the singer and the bass, using chords suggested by the outlines of the continuo part. Almost all music in the period 1600–1750 includes a continuo – it is one of the most characteristic features of baroque music.

Marais, Sonnerie de Ste Geneviève du mont de Paris

Marin Marais spent his whole life in Paris, most of it as a musician at the royal court. He was famous as a performer on the viola da gamba. This is a bowed string instrument a bit like a violin or cello but with frets on the fingerboard and six strings. The strings are under less tension than those on the modern cello, making the thinner sound you can hear on the recording.

GAM page 13   CD 1 Track 2
Sonnerie de Ste Geneviève du mont de Paris
Marin Marais (1656–1728)

Sonnerie de Ste Geneviève du mont de Paris was published in 1723 and is a showpiece for a member of the viola da gamba family called the bass viol. Marais exploits the entire range of the instrument, from the lowest open string (D at the start of bar 31) to the high E at the start of bar 197. Double-stopping (playing two notes at the same time) is required in bars 23–28. In contrast, the violin part is less showy and narrower in range, while the accompaniment is limited to a one-bar ground bass. This is a continuo part and it is realised on a harpsichord (minim–crotchet chords at the start) and theorbo (from bar 23 onwards). These instruments play chords indicated by the numbers and other symbols printed above the bass part (this is known as a figured bass). The numbers in boxes below the stave are not part of the original piece – they refer to the work on page 24 of *GAM*, that we shall discuss later.

Sonnerie is French for 'chimes'; and *Ste Geneviève du mont* is a parish church on the left bank of the River Seine in Paris.

Note that the instruments on the CD are tuned a semitone lower than modern ones.

A theorbo is a very large lute.

The ground bass consists of three crotchets (D–F–E) and in most bars the harmony simply alternates between chords I and V. The key is D minor at the start, despite the lack of a key signature. A little variety is produced by sections in A minor (bars 171–206) and F major (bars 207–251), after which the music returns to D minor until the end. Variety is also provided by sections in which the violin (but seldom the viola da gamba) is silent.

Most of the French performance directions in the score are observed by the performers on the *GAM* recording: *Légèrement* means 'lightly'; *Grand coup d'archet…* means a striking down-bow …*et pointé* refers to an uneven performance of the quavers (this is known as *notes inégales*); *Doux* (or *D.*) means 'soft'; *Fort* (or *F.*) means 'loud'.

In accordance with the performance practice of the time, some other rhythms are not performed as printed in the score. For example, the ♩. ♪ pattern in the violin part of bars 6 and 7 is played as ♩.. ♪

There is also variety on a smaller scale. For instance, the ground moves to the viola da gamba part at bar 29 where repeated quavers replace the original crotchets. This process of splitting a melody into shorter note values was called 'divisions' and you can see more complex examples in the viola da gamba part at bars 49–52 and 93–98. But even when the ground seems to disappear (such as in bars 63–64), three pitches are still there.

Repetition is also a feature of the upper parts, often in the form of a four-bar phrase that is immediately repeated, sometimes with a small amount of variation (eg compare the violin part in bars 5–9 with that in bars 9–12). The overall impression is one of hypnotic repetition, just as it is in another ground-bass piece of the mid-baroque period, Pachelbel's famous *Kanon* in D.

Martland, Re-mix

GAM page 24   CD1 Track 3
Re-mix
Martland (b. 1959)

This modern version of *Sonnerie*, scored for jazz/rock ensemble was created by Steve Martland and is in his characteristic 'crossover' style that draws on elements from jazz, rock and classical music. The mechanical nature of Marais' piece makes it easy to produce a collage of the various phrases from the original. In addition to the explanation on page 24 of *GAM* you might like to notice:

◆ the sax glissandi between A and D in the first phrase and at about 0:15 and 0:20 on track 3 of the anthology CD

◆ the use of **swung quavers**

◆ the nine statements of A–G–F starting at 0:53

◆ Martland's 'divisions' of the ground from 1:07–1:14 (quaver octaves)

◆ the imitation of Marais' falling scale figure (bars 37–38) from 1:19

◆ the piano 'divisions' from 1:56 in which bar 63 of the *Sonnerie* is repeated 20 times with a crescendo

◆ the terrific increase in excitement brought about by the combination of several different motifs in the final minute of the piece

◆ that Marais' one-bar ostinato runs right through the piece in the bass parts (this really is a ground-bass composition!)

◆ that *Re-mix* gets gradually faster in tempo throughout, creating a frenzy of excitement

◆ that *Re-mix* remains in D minor throughout

◆ that *Re-mix* is three minutes shorter than *Sonnerie* and a lot more fun!

❓ Test yourself on ground bass

1. 'Here the deities approve' is taken from a longer work. What type of work is it?..

....

....

2. What is meant by the term continuo?.....................................
    ....
    ....

3. Which of the following best describes the speed of 'Here the deities approve'?

    Adagio   Andante   Allegro   Presto

4. How does Marais vary the ground bass in *Sonnerie de Ste Geneviève*?

    ....
    ....
    ....

5. Listen to tracks 2 and 3 on *GAM* CD1. State which aspects of Marais' *Sonnerie* identify it as a work from the baroque period and which aspects of Martland's *Re-mix* belong to the 20th century. ....

    ....
    ....
    ....
    ....

6. Which do you prefer, Marais' original version or Martland's arrangement? Give three reasons for your choice.

    ....
    ....
    ....

In questions like this you will not get marks for saying 'it sounds better'. You must give detailed musical reasons. For instance, you might prefer Marais' *Sonnerie* because it is played on original instruments, has clearer textures and has more variety of key.

Performing and composing

Try performing or sequencing Pachelbel's *Kanon*. Scores are readily available (simplified but free on http://www.8notes.com) and scores and sequencing directions are given in *Music in Sequence* (by William Lloyd and Paul Terry, Music Sales, ISBN 0-9517214-0-2).

Compose a ground bass using only three pitches, then add two different melodies to it (with or without melodic sequences).

Variations

We have already discussed one type of variation form – the ground bass. The chaconne and passacaglia can both be composed on a ground bass for the whole, or part of a movement. Despite the terms' differing origins, baroque composers used the titles 'chaconne' and 'passacaglia' as if they were interchangeable.

Originally a dance, a chaconne is a continuous set of variations built upon a repeating bass and/or a repeating chord progression. It is usually in slow $\frac{3}{4}$ time. The most famous chaconne of all is the monumental set of 62 variations that comes at the end of Bach's Partita (suite) in D minor for unaccompanied violin (1720). The theme is the chord progression heard in the first four bars (Example 5a). Subtle changes are made to this pattern, but it is always four bars long, always begins on chord I and always ends with a perfect

Chaconne and passacaglia

The most famous passacaglia is also by Bach – his majestic Passacaglia in C minor for organ.

Benjamin Schmid's recording of the *Partita in D minor* is available on *Classics 74321721132*.

You will find longer extracts from this chaconne in *RDMS* A95–A98.

cadence (compare Examples 5a and 5b). Notice that Bach writes three- and four-part chords. Most are impossible on a modern violin, so instead you will hear rapid arpeggios (or similar effects) with just one or two chord-notes sustained (as in the first bar of Example 5b). One way of creating variety in a chaconne is to introduce a block of variations in the tonic major (or the tonic minor if the main key is major). Example 5c is the first of 19 variations in D major that forms a contrasting section between the D-minor tonality of the first 33 variations and the last 12 variations.

Example 5   J S Bach, extracts from Chaconne in D minor (from BWV 1004)

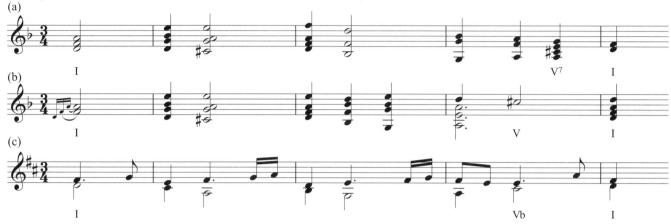

Canonic variations

Canonic variations are not as common as the chaconne and passacaglia, but some of the finest sets of variations written in the 18th and 19th centuries employ this technique. They are of two types. In the first the theme is presented in one part closely followed by the same theme repeated in another part (like a round, such as *Three Blind Mice*). The outer parts of Bach's organ prelude 'Christus, der uns selig macht' ('Christ who makes us blessed') from the *Little Organ Book* form a **canon** using the original chorale melody.

A complete chorale prelude based on the famous carol *In dulci jubilo* can be found on track A94 of *RDMS*. Both the carol melody and the other two parts are in canon throughout all but the last few bars.

Example 6   J S Bach, opening bars from the chorale prelude 'Christus, der uns selig macht', BWV 620

The *Goldberg Variations* (1742) were written for harpsichord but you can also hear performances and recordings on the modern piano. The most famous recording was made by the Canadian pianist Glenn Gould but there are plenty of other good recordings to choose from. Ralph Kirkpatrick's recording of the *Goldberg Variations* is available on *Classikon 4394652*.

In the second type of canonic variation the canon is independent of the theme. In Bach's monumental *Goldberg Variations* the 'theme' is the harmony of a complete binary-form movement. In Variation 12 (See Example 7) Bach uses the same bass as the theme except that three crotchets fill each bar instead of one dotted minim (compare the two bass parts shown below). Above this Bach has written an independent 'canon by **inversion**' (if you compare the two upper parts you should be able to work out what this term means).

Example 7 J S Bach, opening bars of Variation 12 from the *Goldberg Variations*, BWV 988

Variation 30 of the *Goldberg Variations* is a quodlibet, a composition in which several well-known tunes are combined. In this particular quodlibet two tunes are cleverly combined with the bars and harmonies of Bach's theme.

A much simpler type of variation that was very common in the baroque era was the **double**. This French term was used throughout Europe to mean a variation in which each of the notes of the original melody is broken up into two or more faster notes. In the following examples, taken from a gavotte by Handel, you will see that the pitches of the rising scale of the theme are kept in each variation, but more and more decorations are added to them. This is a good example of repetition (in the pitches of the theme), and contrast (in the systematic addition of shorter and shorter note values).

The first half of the theme, the first half of Variation 30 and the two tunes of the quodlibet are recorded on tracks B1, B2 and B3 of *RDMS*.

Double

Longer extracts from this gavotte (with the bass parts) are played on *RDMS* B18.

Example 8 Handel, extracts from the Gavotte in the Keyboard Suite in G, HWV 441

Another simple type of variation technique is to use different accompaniments to the same theme in each variation. The most famous example is the second movement of Haydn's 'Emperor' Quartet, Op. 76, No. 3. The theme is shown *right*. The 'Emperor' of the quartet's nickname was Joseph II of Austria.

In the theme this famous melody is introduced by the first violin with a **homophonic** accompaniment provided by the other strings. In the first variation the second violin plays the theme accompanied by a contrasting countermelody in semiquavers on the first violin. The theme is played by the cello in the second variation while the violins provide a variety of countermelodies and the viola provides essential bass notes. In the third variation the viola melody is accompanied by independent melodies in the other three parts. Up

The Lindsay Quartet's recording of the *Emperor* Quartet is available on *ASV CDDCA1076*.

You may recognise the above as the opening a hymn tune called *Austria* ('Glorious things of thee are spoken'). The tune is also the national anthem of Germany.

to this point there has been a gradual increase in the complexity of the textures: homophony in the theme, two-part counterpoint in the first variation, three-part counterpoint with long bass notes in the second variation, and four-part counterpoint in three bars of the third variation. The climax is reserved for the fourth variation in which the theme returns to the first violin (with some phrases transposed an octave higher), but the sumptuous chromatic harmonies are entirely new.

Beethoven, Diabelli Variations

GAM page 25　　　CD1 Tracks 4–8
Diabelli Variations:
Theme and Variations 1–4
Beethoven (1770–1827)

In 1819 the composer Diabelli had the idea of inviting a large number of composers to contribute one variation each to a theme that he had composed in order to produce an album of contemporary piano music. Beethoven, not content with a single variation, wrote a set of 33, which were published in 1823. Diabelli's theme, and the first four of Beethoven's variations, are printed in *GAM*. All of the variation techniques we have discussed so far can be found in Beethoven's *Thirty-three Variations on a Waltz by Diabelli*. Just as Bach's *Goldberg Variations* sum up baroque variation techniques, so Beethoven's monumental *Diabelli Variations* sum up classical variation techniques (and point the way forward to romantic variations).

You may be surprised by the simplicity of the theme, but simplicity is a virtue in this context because it allows the composer more scope than would be possible with a more sophisticated theme. Diabelli's original waltz is in binary (AB) form. The first half is 16 bars long and modulates at the end to a perfect cadence in the dominant key of G major. The second half is also 16 bars long and begins and ends in the tonic key of C major. Both halves fall into four four-bar phrases and both contain modulating sequences. Beethoven adheres to this overall plan in the four variations that follow, but each exploits aspects of the theme in different ways and each has a distinctly different character.

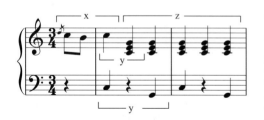

Three elements from the start of the theme are labelled *left*. It starts with a four-note figure (x) rather like a turn. This is followed by a falling 4th from tonic to dominant (y), which is also heard in the bass. The third (z) simply consists of repeated tonic triads.

In Variation 1 Beethoven transforms Diabelli's waltz into a pompous march. The tempo is slower (*maestoso*) and the metre has been changed from $\frac{3}{4}$ to $\frac{4}{4}$. Motifs y and z are retained, but in the bass the descending 4th of y is filled-in with a scale in octaves that clashes with the right-hand chords. The keys are more wide-ranging and the chords are often more complex than those in the theme.

Variation 2 is characterised by continuous offbeat quavers in the right hand, but their melodic shape is derived from x (see *left*). Against these, the repeated triads of z have been moved to the bass. The opening melody of the minuet-like Variation 3 is formed from two falling 4ths (motif y, in fact), while Variation 4 opens with a motif based on a rising then falling 4th, treated in imitation.

Try to listen to a recording of some of the other variations. Beethoven has great fun with Diabelli's waltz. For instance, the C-major triads (z) are mercilessly repeated time and again in Variation 21, while the apparently insignificant opening turn (x) totally dominates Variations 9, 11 and 12.

Paganini, Twenty-four Caprices, Op. 1, No. 24

Listen to the theme and variations from Paganini's Twenty-four Caprices, Op. 1. The harmony implied by the theme becomes explicit in Variation 8. In the first four bars it is a simple alternation of chords I and V in A minor. The second section begins with a segment of a circle of 5ths on the bass notes A–D–G–C and ends with a conventional cadence formula (basically IIb–I–IV–V–I in A minor). Write out the bass of this binary-form harmonic progression, then try to compose your own melody to fit with it. If you succeed in this endeavour your variations should be a piece of cake!

GAM page 30   CD1 Tracks 9–21
Twenty-four Caprices, Op. 1, No. 24
Paganini (1782–1840)

Test yourself on variations

Listen to the fourth movement of Schubert's *Trout* Quintet and answer the following questions.

The Vienna Octet's recording of the *Trout* Quintet is available on *Classic Sound 4486022*.

1. Four of the instruments are piano, violin, viola and cello. What is the fifth instrument in this quintet?.....................................

2. Which instrument does not play in the theme?.........................

3. Write the number of the variation by each of these descriptions:
    (a) A variation with the theme played in octaves on the piano. ....
    (b) A variation with the theme in the bass. ....
    (c) A variation in which only the violin plays triplets. ....
    (d) A variation in a major key that is not the tonic. ....

Composing

Choose a short and simple tune (eg *Three Blind Mice*) and write your own set of variations on it. To get started you could try some of the techniques listed on page 30. But try to be adventurous and give each variation its own character – one could be a jazz waltz, another might develop just one idea from the theme in canon.

As an exercise each member of your group could contribute one variation each on the same theme, just as Diabelli intended for his waltz. Bur remember that such group compositions cannot be submitted as an actual GCSE composition.

Rondo

A **rondo** is a form in which a principal theme (A) alternates with contrasting sections called **episodes** (B, C, D etc) giving a structure such as ABACA. Example 9 shows the melody of a *rondeau* (French for rondo) written by Elisabeth Jacquet de la Guerre and published in 1707 (ornaments have been omitted).

A complete score (with ornaments) and recording of Jacquet de la Guerre's rondeau can be found in *RDMS*.

Example 9   Jacquet de la Guerre, rondeau from *Pièces de clavecin*

The rondo theme (or refrain) is in the key of G minor and consists of two four-bar phrases, the first ending with an imperfect cadence (II–V), the second with a perfect cadence (V–I). The first episode B is in the contrasting key of B♭ major (the relative major) until the last few bars where it rapidly modulates to an imperfect cadence in G minor ready for an exact repetition of the refrain (shown by the letter A in a box). The second episode begins in G minor but soon moves through F major to D minor. Finally the refrain (A) is repeated with decorative quavers followed by a little coda starting in bar 41, which is a repeat of bars 37–41. Thus the form can be represented as:

A (G minor)	B (contrasting keys)	A (G minor)	C (contrasting keys)	A (G minor)

Vivaldi, The Four Seasons: 'Autumn', movement III

Ritornello form

GAM page 34   CD1 Track 22
The Four Seasons: 'Autumn', movement III
Vivaldi (1678–1741)

Ritornello form originated in the instrumental sections of baroque arias. (Look back to the beginning of this chapter and reread the notes on 'He was despised' from Handel's *Messiah*.) The principle of alternating tutti and solo passages was exploited to the full in many of the fast movements of Vivaldi's concertos. The last movement of 'Autumn', the third concerto of his set of four solo concertos called *The Four Seasons* (published c.1725), is one of the clearest examples of the form. Instead of a singer a violinist takes the starring role, and the form differs from the French *rondeau* in that the tutti refrain (or ritornello) is often transposed and fragmented after its first appearance. Although there are similarities between rondo and ritornello form, the two are usually quite distinct. In particular the sections in a rondo are often longer and more self-contained than those in a ritornello-form movement. However the structure of this particular ritornello-form movment is similar to that of a rondo.

The movement shown in *GAM* is about hunting. Hunting horns, like all horns in Vivaldi's time, had no valves, so they were only capable of playing a limited range of pitches. Horns in F could play F, G, A, Bb, C, D, Eb and F on the treble stave. These are precisely the pitches Vivaldi uses for the melody of bars 1–13 (which we will identify as x^1 from now on). The remainder of the opening ritornello consists of repetitions of the two-bar motif first heard in bars 14–15 (we will identify this as motif y) and a version of the 'horn motif' (which we will identify as motif x^2) ending with perfect cadences in bars 24–25 and 28–29. The whole ritornello is never again repeated in full, but it contains all the melodic materials that are used in the ritornellos that punctuate the violin solo in the rest of the movement.

Remember the symbols we have used to identify the three sections of the ritornello as you read the following outline of the whole movement.

A1 (bars 1–29): Complete ritornello in F major.

B (bars 30–41): First episode. F major. The rhythms of both the solo violin (using double-stopping) and *basso continuo* (Bc. in the score) come from motif y.

A2 (bars 42–49^1): Ritornello. F major. Constructed from one phrase of x^1 and one phrase of x^2 from the opening ritornello.

C (bars 49–69): Second episode. F major modulating to a dominant pedal in C major (bars 59–68) by means of a sequence passing through C major (bars 55–56) and D minor (bars 57–58).

In bar 60 the performance direction *segue* means that the broken-chord figures of bar 59 should be maintained until the end of the solo (bar 68).

A3 (bars 69–76): Ritornello. C major.

D (bars 76–96): Third episode. C major. The solo violin represents the fleeing beast, and tutti strings complete the picture by their fierce scrubbing in bars 84–85 and 94–95.

A4 (bars 97–104). Ritornello. C major. A repeat of bars 69–75.

E (bars 104–115). Fourth episode. C major modulating to F major using the triplet figures from the third episode (bars 76–81).

A5 (bars 116–123). Ritornello. F major. A repeat of bars 1–8.

F (bars 123–141). Fifth episode. F major.

A6 (bars 142–157). Ritornello. F major.

Classical rondo forms

Unlike the ritornellos in baroque ritornello form, the refrains in classical rondo forms are usually all in the same key. They are most often lightweight movements used as cheerful finales in multi-movement works such as sonatas, symphonies and concertos.

Weber, Clarinet Quintet in B♭: movement IV

GAM page 40   CD1 Track 23
Clarinet Quintet in B♭: movement IV
Weber

If the scale and complexity of this movement reminds you of sonata-form movements you may have come across this is not surprising, for this is an example of a hybrid structure known as sonata-rondo form.

Weber's Clarinet Quintet is noticeable for the brilliant quality of writing for the clarinet. The clarinettist is in fact so prominent in the piece and is given so many opportunities to shine that you might wonder whether this is true 'chamber music'. Is the clarinettist really a member of a small group or are they really the soloist in a miniature concerto designed to allow them to show off what they and their instrument can do?

Note for example the use of the clarinet's full range. Weber has written for the 'clarino' range of the top notes, the 'throat' notes of the middle, and the darker, warmer sound of the bass notes of the 'chalumeau' range. He has also used many of the clarinet's most characteristic sounds: as you listen to the piece do you spot the burbling arpeggios, the cantabile melodies and the brilliant scales?

The long binary-form rondo theme is in B♭ major (bars 1–31). The first section (A) of the binary structure (bars 1–10) ends on the dominant (bar 10, beat 2). The second section (B) begins with a passage that modulates through D♭ major to chord V^7 of B♭ major (bar 23, beat 2), then bars 3–7 of A are repeated, the whole rondo theme ending with the perfect cadence in B♭ major in bar 31. A transition (bars 32–67) modulates from B♭ major to V^7 of F major (bars 55–67). Complete silence alerts us to the entry of the first episode (bars 69–118) which is the dominant key of F major. At the last moment does the clarinet announces an arpeggio of V^7 of B♭ major (bars 117–118) ready for the return of the rondo theme (bars 119–155) the last few bars of which are modified and extended to link with the central episode (bars 156–282). This huge section passes through many keys and revisits some of the thematic materials we have already heard. After another dramatic silence (bar 283) an abridged version of the rondo theme (bars 284–299) leads directly into a recapitulation of the first episode transposed to the tonic (bars 300–355 = bars 69–104 with slight modifications). The coda (bars 335–387) never leaves the tonic key.

There is more than one way to analyse the music. The table on page 40 of GAM shows one way of tackling the first half of this complex movement, but it may be better to take a more global view:

A	link	B	A	C	A	B	Coda
(1–31)	(32–67)	(69–118)	(119–155)	(156–282)	(284–299)	(300–335)	(335–387)

Test yourself on rondo form

1. Explain what is meant by the terms 'refrain' and 'episode' in a rondo. ....
....
....

2. In Vivaldi's 'Autumn' (movement III):

    (i)   How does the ritornello in bars 69–76 differ from the
          ritornello in bars 42–49? ....

          ....

    (ii) Where in the third episode (bars 76–96) is there a
          sequence like the one in the second episode (bars 49–69)?
          In what ways do they differ? ....

          ....

          ....

          ....

    (iii) How does Vivaldi represent the death of the beast in the
          fifth episode (bars 123–141)? ....

          ....

          ....

3. In what way does the texture of Weber's Rondo bars 156–169
    differ from all other textures in this rondo? ....

    ....

    ....

    ....

Composing

Add a simple bass part to the melody of Jacquet de la Guerre's refrain
(bars 0–8). If you think of your bass melodically there will be no need
for complete chords (the original *rondeau* is in two parts except at a
couple of the cadences). Now compose your own episodes. You could
use Jacquet de la Guerre's key schemes or simpler schemes of your
own devising.

Serialism

Arnold Schönberg (1874–1951) was born in German-speaking Vienna. After emigrating to the USA in 1933 he changed the spelling of his surname to Schoenberg.

Camerata Bern's recording of *Verklärte Nacht* is available on *ECM New Series 4657782*.

Towards the end of the 19th century, romantic composers such as Wagner often used so many discords and chromatic notes to express intense emotion that it is impossible to say what key the music is in. Arnold Schoenberg's early compositions, such as his string sextet *Verklärte Nacht* (Transfigured Night, 1899), were written in a lush Wagnerian style of this sort. Example 1 shows how keys can still be heard in this piece – there are tonic and dominant-7th chords of D minor in the first and last bars – but the three bars between them are so chromatic and discordant that it is impossible to say what key they are in. In these bars the music has no **tonality** – it is **atonal**.

Example 1 Schoenberg, *Verklärte Nacht* (1899)

In later compositions Schoenberg abandoned tonality altogether (see Example 2). But the trouble is that, no matter how expressive atonal music may be, it is hard to compose long instrumental movements without the binding force of tonality. A new musical principle was needed.

Example 2 Schoenberg, *Six Little Pieces for Piano*, Op. 19, No. 6 (1911)

Tone row
After much trial and error Schoenberg discovered that if the 12 chromatic pitches are arranged in a particular order, without repetition, and if this order (or strictly limited variants of it) is used systematically it is possible to compose long movements without the need for contrasting keys. Any order of 12 chromatic pitches of this sort is called a **tone row** or note row. The original tone row from which a composition springs is known as the **basic series**, and it is from this term that the word 'serialism' derives ('prime order' means the same as 'basic series' and is now a more common term). Schoenberg's *Suite for Piano* (1923) was his first extended work to be based on a single 12-note row.

Independently one of Schoenberg's colleagues, Josef Hauer, evolved his own type of serial technique. Example 3 comes at the beginning of a song Hauer composed in 1922. Voice and piano are in octaves with no supporting harmony.

Example 3 Hauer, 'Hälfte des Lebens', from *Hölderlin-Lieder*, Op. 21

In this unaccompanied melody it is easy to hear how the 12 notes of a chromatic scale have been arranged to form the four three-note motifs or 'cells' identified by the letters A, B, C and D:

Notice that in Example 3 cells A and B rise then fall a tone or semitone, while cells C and D reverse this order by first falling then rising a tone or semitone (an example of melodic **inversion**).

Stravinsky, Fanfare for a New Theatre

Patterns such as these can often be found in more complex serial compositions, but you must not expect them to be as obvious to the ear and eye as Hauer's prime order is. Example 4 shows the first statement of the prime order of the tone row in Stravinsky's *Fanfare for a New Theatre*.

> *GAM page 70* CD2 Track 2
> *Fanfare for a New Theatre*
> Stravinsky (1882–1971)

Example 4 Stravinsky, *Fanfare for a New Theatre*

Trumpet 2, bar 2

It looks and sounds more complicated than the row in Example 3 because there is no regular metrical pattern and the four big leaps add to the jerky effect of the melody.

Rhythm

Even when there is a time signature at the start of a serial composition the rhythms are often so complex that it is impossible to feel a regular pulse. The basic rhythmic unit of the *Fanfare* is a quaver, but it is so short (less than half a second long) that it does not suggest a pulse. Instead we hear rhythmic cells made up of various groupings of the basic quaver unit.

The most immediately obvious rhythmic feature of Stravinsky's piece is rapid repeated notes. They are characteristic of nearly all brass fanfares (think of the way Mendelssohn's 'Wedding March' begins), and they are particularly effective on trumpets, especially when the techniques of double and triple tonguing are used.

It is these repeated-note rhythms, crammed into 30 seconds of music, that give the fanfare the breathtaking sense of excitement that was needed for the opening ceremony of the Lincoln Square Dance Theatre in New York in 1964.

Structure

The **prime order** is the original note row in a serial composition, and it is made up of a combination of the 12 chromatic pitch classes. Can you see how Example 4 relates to Example 5? It is common practice for all of the notes in the row to be sounded once before any of the notes are repeated. The prime order is often varied

The note-row variations mentioned here are often abbreviated to P (prime order), I (inverted order), R (retrograde order) and RI (retrograde inversion).

and manipulated, and there are a number of standard ways to treat this series.

Example 5

Prime order without repetition or different octaves

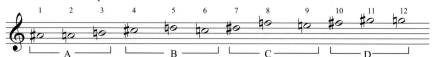

An **inverted order** is the prime order played upside down. For example, if the prime order begins with a rising semitone, the inverted order would begin with a falling semitone, and so on. You can see this if you compare the prime order in Example 5 with the inverted order in Example 6. In the *Fanfare* the inverted order is played by the second trumpet starting on the A♯ in the fourth system and by the first trumpet starting on the repeated A♯s in the last system.

Example 6

Inverted order

When the prime order is sounded backwards, this is known as the **retrograde order** (see Example 7). It is played by the first trumpet in the third system of the *Fanfare*.

Example 7

Retrograde order

The retrograde inversion could be described as the prime order played backwards and upside down!

If the retrograde order is played upside down, it is known as a **retrograde inversion**. Look at the retrograde inversion in Example 8 and see if you can find an example of this in Stravinsky's score (*GAM*, page 70). Clue: it appears in the second trumpet part (but remember that the notes can appear in different octaves).

Example 8

Retrograde inversion

These various note rows can be shifted up or down by any interval from one to 11 semitones. This is called **transposition**. In Example 9 you can see RI$_6$ of Stravinsky's row. This is the sixth transposition of the retrograde inversion that the first trumpet plays in the fourth system of the *Fanfare*.

Remember that the $_6$ of RI$_6$ refers to semitones not tones.

Example 9

RI$_6$

Note rows are also subject to octave displacement (where the pitches can be sounded in any octave) and repetition.

Verticalisation

Making chords from a tone row is called verticalisation. Here is an extract from the second movement of Stravinsky's *Canticum Sacrum* (1955):

Example 9 Stravinsky, *Canticum Sacrum*

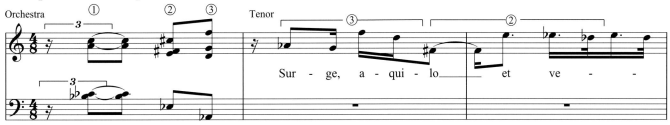

The three chords at the start (labelled 1, 2 and 3) come from the prime order (in this case the tenor solo) played backwards (the retrograde order). Notice that the C♭ in chord 1 is notated as B♮ in the melody of bar 4, and that the C♯ of chord 2 is notated as D♭ in the melody of bar 3. Such enharmonic spellings are common in serial music. Because of this it is better to think of intervals between pitches in a tone row in terms of how many semitones apart they are, rather than as being a minor 3rd, perfect 4th and so on. Notice too that in bars 3–4 of Example 9 and throughout the *Fanfare* Stravinsky (like Schoenberg before him) disregards the strict serial 'rule' that individual pitches of a note row should not be repeated until the row has been completed.

Westminster Cathedral Choir's recording of *Canticum Sacrum* is available on *Hyperion CDA66437*.

Webern, Variations for Piano, Op. 27: movement II

Here is the prime order (P_0) of the tone row on which Webern based his Variations for Piano:

GAM page 69   CD2 Track 1
Variations for Piano, Op. 27:
movement II
Webern (1883–1945)

In the second movement we first hear it transposed up four semitones (P_4):

The first nine notes of P_4 appear on the upper stave of bars 0–4 and the last three on the lower stave in bars 5–6[1] (see Example 14 on page 56). We also hear an inversion of the tone row in these opening bars. Here is the original tone row inverted (I_0):

And here it is transposed up six semitones (I^6):

Webern uses the first nine notes of I₆ on the lower stave in bars 0–6. Like P₄ it then swaps staves, so the last three notes appear on the upper stave of bars 5–6. We can see how P₄ and I₆ are used together in these first six bars – notice the use of verticalisation (shown by the box at E). Take care to read the clefs and leger lines correctly and remember that the notes of the row can appear in any octave:

Example 14 Webern, Variations for Piano, movement II

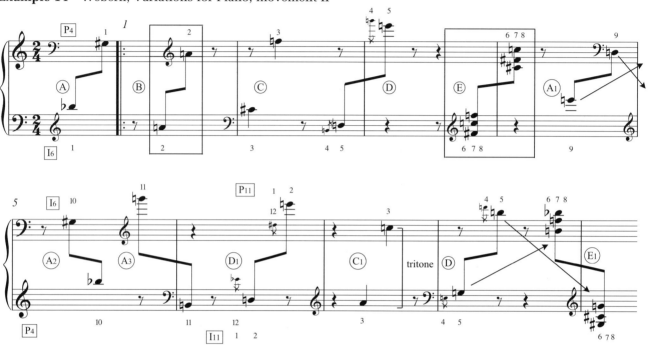

In bar 6 the last note of I₆ (D♯) becomes the first note of P₁₁. In the same way the last note of P₄ (E♭) becomes the first note of I₁₁. These two rows change staves in bar 8 and they both end in bar 11. Notice that notes 6, 7 and 8 are used to form similar chords to those in bars 3–4 and that similar rhythms reflect those in bars 0–6.

Symmetry is also apparent in the second half of this binary-form piece – again, previous rhythms are re-used, and again the chords are formed from notes 6, 7 and 8 of the rows currently in force. P₆ is used on the lower stave and I₄ on the upper – mirroring the use of P₄ and I₆ at the start. Both of these begin on the last beat of bar 11 and again overlap with the last notes of the previous rows. Finally P₉ and I₁ are used for the last 24 notes of the piece. If you want to trace this for yourself, be careful in bars 17–18, where there is some complicated swapping of staves.

In this movement Webern has used only the prime order and its inversion, although both are transposed to various pitch levels. The sparse texture and very wide leaps (necessitating frequent changes of clef) are characteristic of many serialist pieces.

Also typical of Webern's music is the use of canon – in particular, canon by inversion. First we need to see what this means, using a much simpler type of music as an example.

Canonic structure

When a melody is copied in inverted form by another part after a short interval of time the two parts form a canon by inversion.

Persuade a few friends to sing just the alto and bass parts of Example 15: this is a straightforward canon at the octave with the bass singing the same melody as the alto, but an octave lower and four bars later.

Example 15   Anonymous, *Three Blind Mice*

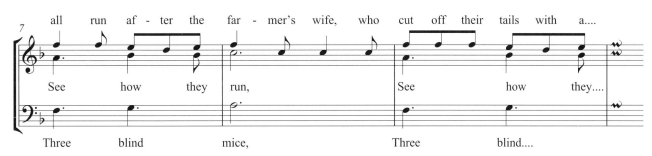

Now sing the treble and alto parts: this is a canon by inversion because the alto part is a melodic inversion of the soprano part. (You could now sing all three parts of Example 15, then try adding a fourth part – an inversion perhaps? – and see what happens if you continue the round with each voice going back to the beginning immediately after the last dotted minim.) The whole of Example 14 – and, indeed, the whole movement – is a canon by inversion, but it differs from the soprano and alto parts of Example 15 in three important ways:

✦ Webern's canonic melodies are characterised by huge leaps

✦ Webern's canonic melodies are intertwined

✦ notes 6–8 of both of Webern's melodies are verticalised to form three-note chords.

All three factors combined with the atonal style make it impossible to recognise the canon by ear.

Motivic structure

Did you notice that *Three Blind Mice* is made up of three distinct motifs, each of them two bars long? They are united by key and metre, but they are contrasted in pitch and rhythm. Webern cannot rely on the binding force of tonality, and, although Example 14 is notated in $\frac{2}{4}$ time, constant syncopation makes it difficult to detect a regular pulse. Instead Webern achieves both unity and variety by his manipulation of five strongly characterised motifs which are deployed throughout the movement. In Example 14 we have labelled these motifs with capital letters. These are their characteristic features:

✦ Motif A consists of two quavers of different pitches

✦ Motif B consists of two quavers of the same pitch

+ Motif C consists of two overlapping crotchets of different pitches
+ Motif D consists of two quavers of different pitches ornamented with grace notes
+ Motif E consists of two closely related three-note chords.

These are the characteristics that make the last seven motifs of Example 14 similar to the first five (the little numbers after the letters indicate varied repeats). Some are more closely related than others. For instance, A^2 is an inversion of A using the same **pitch classes**. You should now go through the whole movement to see how many different versions of these five motifs you can find.

Texture, articulation and dynamics

If you found this movement difficult to understand look instead at bars 1–23 of the third movement from the same set of variations printed in *SM*, page 110.

Although we have noticed the theoretical canon that runs through the second movement of Webern's Variations for Piano what is heard is **monophony** – a single melodic line with no accompaniment. The only exceptions are the brief chordal textures in bars 3–4, 8–9, 15 and 19–20. Alternatively you might feel that the intervals between successive notes are so huge that what you hear are random-sounding pin-pricks of sound scattered throughout a range of nearly four octaves (motif A^3 in Example 14 consists of the highest and lowest pitches used in this movement). If this is how you hear the music you could equally well describe the texture as **pointillist** (made up of 'points' of sound like the dots of paint in some early 20th-century French paintings).

If you don't understand the signs listen to the music. If you still don't understand (and the music does flash past at a tremendous speed) ask your teacher to explain what they mean.

There are five different ways of articulating notes ranging from the legato phrasing of motif A (indicated by a slur) to the staccato articulation of motif B. See if you can find the three other types of articulation.

When all these elements are combined the texture changes in fractions of a second producing a dazzling effect that we can enjoy whether or not we understand the complex compositional processes that lie beneath the glinting surface of the music.

Form

The movement is laid out like a baroque binary-form movement, complete with repeats. But when we discussed ternary form in Area of Study 1 we noticed that the most important element that gave shape to the music was tonality. As Webern cannot make use of this resource, he resorts to motifs as a substitute for tonality. In particular exact repetitions mark the beginning and end of sections. Motif A, for instance comes unaltered at the end of both sections (bars 11 and 22), while the easily recognised repeated A♮ of motif B appears twice within each section (bars 1, 9, 13 and 19). Aurally the repetitions of the grace notes in motif D and the chords in motif E are the most obvious landmarks, but notice how they are subtly varied each time they appear.

Test yourself on serial music

1. Ring the word that best describes serial music:

   Tonal   Diatonic   Atonal   Romantic   Modal

2. What is meant by a 'prime order'? ....
   ....

3. What is verticalisation?..
    ....

Performing

Schoenberg's *Six Little Pieces for Piano*, mentioned above, are fairly easy atonal (though not serialist) music. Kazimierz Serocki's *Suite of Preludes* (1952) includes the very easy No. 5 (PWM 5611). Robert Moevs' *Rondo* for piano (Presser/Alfred Kalmus) would also be worth looking at.

Composing

Try composing a short serial composition. There are a number of stages to this:

✦ First you must decide on your note row. If this causes you difficulty, try writing out the 12 notes of a chromatic scale on a series of pieces of paper or cards. Then arrange them in patterns (look at the Hauer Example 3 and notice the patterns he uses). For instance, you could start with a falling semitone (say, C to B) and then keep repeating this pattern a tone higher. This would give C, B, D, C♯, E, E♭, F♯, F♮, A♭, G, B♭, A♮. For an alternative symmetrical pattern you could construct a note row from rising minor 3rds: start with C, E♭, F♯ and A, then repeat these notes a semitone higher (C♯, E, G and B♭) and finally a semitone higher still (D, F, G♯ and B). Or you could try notes that are four semitones apart – start with C, E, G♯ and then transpose this pattern in semitones to complete the row (C♯, F, A, then D, F♯, B♭, and finally E♭, G, B). Note rows do not have to be symmetrical – these are just a few ideas to help you get started.

✦ Work out the retrograde version of your row (the row backwards), the inverted version (the row upside down), the retrograde inversion (the row backwards and upside down) and if you are feeling really brave, transpose the four versions of your row 11 times, raising each note by one semitone per transposition.

✦ You now will have a lot of melodic material with which to work. Your piece should open with a statement of the note row in its prime order (remember that you can write each pitch class in any octave), and then it is up to you to decide which other melodic idea you use next. To keep it under control, try to make your composition 8–16 bars long, and keep the rhythm fairly simple at this stage – concentrate on using a small number of note-row combinations in a melodically interesting way.

✦ Many composers choose to 'break the rules'. Why not consider reasons and opportunities to do this yourself? For example you might decide to use only the first half of your row for one short passage, then only the second half for a complementary passage.

When writing out a serial composition it is a good idea to put an accidental (♭, ♯ or ♮) before every note, even if not strictly necessary, in order to make your intentions clear.

Experimental music

In 1917 the artist Marcel Duchamp (1887–1968) purchased a urinal from a plumber's merchant in New York, signed it 'R. Mutt', dated it, and entered it for an art exhibition. Two years later he drew moustaches and a goatee beard on a print of Leonardo da Vinci's famous *Mona Lisa*. Both these products of an international experimental movement called Dadaism were meant to be provocative and question the conventions of other, more traditional styles of contemporary art. If you find them shocking now, imagine the effect they had at the end of World War I. Chaos in the trenches was reflected in chaotic art, Dadaism being just one of many 'isms' into which traditional art fragmented in the course of the 20th century. It is significant that John Cage, the most important experimental composer of the century, should have written a composition entitled *Music for Marcel Duchamp* (1947).

Silence

Turn to page 63 for more about silence and performing suggestions.

Today it is possible to see that the serial music of Schoenberg and Berg was really a continuation of 19th-century romanticism, and that the more severe avant-garde serial styles of Webern, Boulez and Stockhausen were an extension of this central tradition of 20th-century art music. For the musical equivalent of Duchamp's enigmatic urinal and iconoclastic *Mona Lisa* we have to wait until 1952 when John Cage's famous *4' 33"* was launched on an unsuspecting audience. It can be 'performed' on any instrument or group of instruments since it consists of three 'movements', each marked with the single word *tacet* (be silent).

Aleatoric music

The term aleatoric is taken from a Latin word meaning 'dependent on the throw of dice'.

All aleatoric effects mentioned can be heard on track C97 of *RDMS*.

Music in which chance plays a significant role is known as **aleatoric** music. It can range from the almost total indeterminacy of *4' 33"* to passages in a piece written in conventional notation in which the performers are allowed considerable latitude within prescribed boundaries.

Part of the score of *Zyklus* is shown in *SM* pages 122–123.

Karlheinz Stockhausen (b. 1928) was one of the most versatile composers of the second half of the 20th century. He worked in serial styles and aleatoric styles, and made full use of the developing resources of electronically generated and manipulated sound. The score of his *Zyklus* (1959) includes staff notation in which lengths of notes are indeterminate. Precise pitches are sometimes indicated, as in the vibraphone parts in the first box and in the triangle. The performance can begin at any point and stop when it has come full circle back to the selected starting point (*Zyklus* means 'cycle'). Another chance element is provided by the treble clefs at the beginning and ends of staves indicating that the music can be turned upside down and played backwards. Finally the musical events within each box can be performed in any order. Piano Sonata No. 3 (1955/1957) by Pierre Boulez (b. 1925) is also notated but players can decide between a number of different routes through the material.

Living Water from Macmillan's *Quickening* can be found on track C97 of *RDMS*. If you don't have access to this work you could listen to the Sanctus from Britten's *War Requiem* (1961). After the soprano solo at the beginning of the fourth movement ('Sanctus Dominus Deus Sabaoth') each part of the eight-part chorus is given up to six notes of indeterminate duration on which to chant the words *Pleni sunt caeli et terra gloria tua* (Heaven and earth are full of your glory).

In bars 9–11 and 23–25 of 'Living Water' from James MacMillan's *Quickening* (1999) headless demisemiquavers in the woodwind and string parts cover a range of imprecise pitches extending from above the treble stave to below the bass stave. This semi-aleatoric notation is accompanied by the performance directions: 'Fast flurry of notes in the direction, range and for the duration roughly indicated, ad lib., *prestissimo possibile, virtuoso, wild, violento, sempre stacc.*' Later in the same movement the sopranos and altos of a large chorus are given a range of pitches, but each individual is instructed to change from one pitch to the next to form a unique chant. The result is a controlled chaos that contrasts and alternates with similarly aleatoric parts for hand bells and tubular bells.

Graphic scores

In addition to staff notation, the score of Stockhausen's *Zyklus* includes graphics that invite aleatoric performance (such as the güiro part). Scores in which the composer uses pictures and diagrams are known as graphic scores. These can use symbols that act in a way similar to conventional notation, for example indicating changes of pitch or giving some guidance about duration, but without being prescriptive. Graphic scores can also set out to look pleasing and to inspire players creativity.

Cardew, Treatise

Treatise (1967) by Stockhausen's pupil Cornelius Cardew consists entirely of pages of graphics which have to be turned into sound by the performers. The score should probably be read, and therefore performed, from left to right. The CD contains two very different performances. Note that track 6 is half the length of track 8 even though they are performances of the same page: Cardew leaves it to the performers to decide how quickly each page should be played.

GAM page 80   CD2 Tracks 6–9
Treatise: pages 190–191
Cornelius Cardew (1936–1981)

The musicians must listen to each other to make a good group-sound – listening is as important as playing. The table below shows *some* of the different choices that the two ensembles on the CD make:

Track 6	Track 8
Clarinet leads with short notes	Sustained note G
String sound very quietly sustained	Piano develops pattern on C minor
Clarinet trill	Wildly improvised wind lines
String glissando up (on the bridge)	Piano: complex cluster chords

Track 7	Track 9
Violin harmonics F♯/A/E	Saxophone very quiet and high notes
Sustained electronic sounds	Sustained string, clarinet and organ notes
Piano chord three times	Chord cluster (everyone) ten times
Clarinet, string and vibraphone	High tinkly sounds and rapid playing

This approximately follows the order in which events occur, but some things happen simultaneously.

Extended vocal techniques

Stripsody (1966) by the singer-composer Cathy Berberian is a piece 'notated' as amusing graphics on three-line staves that suggest the approximate tessitura of notes of definite pitch and of a huge variety of vocal sound effects. These extended vocal effects include the ticking of a clock; the tuning of a radio (with snippets from an opera and a pop song); kissing and eating noises; farmyard animals falling asleep to the accompaniment of Brahms' *Lullaby*; and even a vocal representation of an earthquake.

Tessitura is the range of pitch within which a vocal or instrumental part mostly lies.

You can hear all of these effects in *SM*, which also includes an extract from *Stripsody* (pages 124–125).

Cage, Living Room Music: 'Story'

After *Stripsody* 'Story' from Cage's *Living Room Music* (1940) may seem tame. Childlike simplicity is suggested at the start by a text that begins like a fairy story ('Once upon a time'), but the suggestion that the world is no longer round reminds us of Dadaism and Surrealism. Although it can be performed by amateurs, Cage's consistent exploitation of the percussive possibilities of ordinary speech, together with the literally 'extended vocal technique' of prolonged vowels and consonants, is anything but childish.

GAM page 74   CD2 Track 5
Living Room Music: 'Story'
John Cage (1912–1992)

Extended instrumental techniques are not well illustrated in either *GAM* or *NAM*, but a range can be heard in the following tracks of *RDMS*:

C34 Flutter-tonguing (rolling the letter 'r' while blowing a wind instrument).

C43 A rim shot on a side drum (produced by striking the rim and head simultaneously with one stick, or by placing one stick so that it touches the rim and the head then striking it with the other stick).

C69 Strumming the strings of a viola in the same way the guitar is strummed in C83.

C70 Deliberately playing a quarter of a tone flat on one violin while another violin plays the same notes in tune so that an acidic 'folky' tone is produced.

C71 Snap pizzicato (plucking a string vigorously so it rebounds off the fingerboard), and pizzicato glissando (plucking a string with a finger of the right hand then moving a finger of the left hand up or down the string so the original note slides up or down in pitch).

C90 A cluster of piano harmonics produced by silently depressing a range of keys with one arm then activating the harmonics by loud staccato notes at the bottom of the keyboard.

C94 Plucked strings on a grand piano.

Some of the notation symbols for extended vocal and instrumental techniques are used fairly consistently by living composers. If you want to use them, consult pages 203–213 of Reginald Smith-Brindle's **The New Music**, *Oxford University Press*, second edition.

GAM page 83 CD2 Track 10
Songs from the Hill: 'Wa-lie-oh'
Meredith Monk (b. 1942)

The little circle underneath the note A means a kind of falsetto effect created as the voice is pushed between different registers.

There are six principal rhythmic motifs first heard at the following points:

(a) Bar 1, beats 1–2: an on-beat figure of four semiquavers and a quaver

(b) Bar 5, voice 4: a long note followed by a staccato note

(c) Bar 7, voice 3: a two-quaver figure formed from a monosyllable ('once') divided into two syllables ('won-suh') with syncopation caused by the accent on the second syllable

(d) Bar 8, voice 2: a two-note long–short rhythm that differs from all others because an approximate pitch falls on the vowel ('worl') and is cut short by a percussive consonant ('d')

(e) Bars 14–15: a homorhythmic cadence figure of five notes (ie voices 1, 3 and 4 all have the same rhythm at the same time)

(f) Bars 22–28: motifs distinguished by their triplet figures.

In addition there are long pedal-like notes: the sustained sibilants ('ssss' in bars 22–25 and 'zzz' in bars 26–29).

From the six motifs and variants of them, together with the 'pedals' Cage creates a wide variety of textures including:

✦ monophony in bars 1–4

✦ two-part **cross-rhythms** over a 'pedal' in bars 22–25

✦ three-part rhythmic counterpoint in bars 8–11

✦ four-part rhythmic counterpoint in bars 46–48.

The form of the whole piece is ternary (XYX_1). Both X and Y divide into two seven-bar phrases, the ends of which are marked with double barlines. The end of the first section is marked by the homorhythmic cadence figure of bars 14–15. The middle episode (Y, bars 15–28) is distinguished from X by a return to monophony in the first phrase and the introduction of motif f and pedals in the second phrase. The recapitulation (X_1) begins with a reworking of motifs a, d and b. In bars 39–42 motif c returns, then in the most complex texture of the whole piece, motif f is combined with motifs a, b and c in bar 46.

Monk, Songs from the Hill: 'Wa-lie-oh'

Meredith Monk's 'Wa-lie-oh' from *Songs from the Hill* is an unaccompanied vocal solo with a text of nonsense syllables. But it is a clever piece because it creates a sense of harmony (even though you only hear one note at a time). It makes good use of rhythm as well.

The score shows the main cells (basic musical ideas) in each section, although these are often repeated and modified, and neither pitch nor rhythm is always precisely shown by the notation. At the start the singer first alternates between B and F♯, an interval of a perfect 5th. Gradually other notes are introduced (including a low F♯ and a D♯), so extending the range and giving a sense of B-major harmony. Section 2 begins on a down-beat instead of an up-beat and is restricted to the interval of a major 3rd (B–D♯) until the note A is introduced near the end. This forms the 7th of the B^7 chord that is gradually emerging. The 7th features prominently in the third section, which has the widest vocal range so far (almost two octaves).

Section 4 combines cells from sections 2 and 3, while section 5 introduces several new pitches. The arrows on the accidentals A♭ and G♯ indicate that **microtones** are required (intervals of less than a semitone). In section 6 music from section 2 returns, but note the dramatic effect of the unexpected C♮. After that the music becomes more complicated, descending to a low register at the end of the section. Section 3 is repeated (forming section 7) to end the piece.

The composer describes her piece as being in 'modified rondo form'. This is because a certain section keeps returning. Can you see which?

Test yourself on experimental music

1. Compare the two different interpretations of the extract from *Treatise* by Cornelius Cardew. Which of them relates most closely to the score? Justify your answer. ....
   ....
   ....

2. (a) What new rhythm is introduced in (i) section 5, and (ii) section 6 of 'Wa-lie-oh'? ....
   ....

   (b) What is a cell and how does Monk make use of cells?
   ....
   ....

Performing

You could perform Cage's *4′ 33″* with a group of friends. The three movements are 30″, 2′ 25″ and 1′ 40″ in length. Whoever is chosen to be soloist should walk on stage and then signify the start and end of each movement with a suitable gesture – pianists could open the keyboard cover for the duration of the movement, or other instrumentalists could hold their instrument in playing position for the appropriate length of time. Was there absolute silence? Didn't you begin to notice the sound of your own and your friends' breathing? Could you detect the distant sound of birds singing, or of road traffic, or of a passing aeroplane? Do these sounds constitute music? And do they mean anything? And if they don't mean anything, what is the composer trying to say to us?

Try to create a group performance of one of the pages from *Treatise*. You will need to decide whether each performer responds to single elements on the page (for example the ascending lines) or takes into account the whole of the graphic score.

Before you attempt a performance of 'Story' you might like to try out Ernst Toch's easier *Geographical Fugue* (Mills Music Ltd). Like 'Story', it is scored for four speaking voices. Unlike 'Story' the voices must include high and low women's voices (or trebles and boy altos) and high and low men's voices. Tomasz Sikorski's *Sonant* (PWM 7991) is an example of an approachable aleatoric piece for piano.

Composing

Create a graphic score for an ensemble. When doing this, think about how you envisage the music taking shape. Try and perform some sections of the piece either by singing it, or by using pitched percussion instruments or keyboards.

The way that Britten and MacMillan introduce aleatoric passages in their music (see page 60) and the way in which they have notated these passages could be a model for your work.

Try and compose a piece using only the notes G, C, E and B♭. Divide up your piece into short, clearly defined sections.

Minimalism

But is it new? Listen to *Gymnopédie* No. 3 (1888) by Erik Satie (see *below*) and try to spot some of the minimalist techniques mentioned here.

In music the adjective 'minimalist' was first used in the early 1970s to describe the style of music written by some American composers working in the previous decade (when 'systems music' was a common term for minimalist compositions). Features that were common to minimalist styles of this period were simple repetitive rhythm, diatonic melody, and unmoving or slowly changing harmony.

Like many other creative figures from the 1960s Stockhausen was drawn to seek refuge from the complexities of western culture in the contemplative religions of the far east. In his *Stimmung* ('Tuning', 1968) six singers quietly chant mystical texts into microphones. As the music slowly transforms they explore the resonances of their vocal cavities and gradually move closer to the exact pitches of the chord shown *above*. This chord is played electronically, just loud enough for the singers to hear as a reference point for pitch.

It persists unchanged for 75 minutes while each performer sings repeated words or vowel sounds on one of the pitches before changing to another of the chord notes.

Can you see that the static chord in *Stimmung* consists of a major triad (B♭–D–F) plus a minor 7th (A♭) and major 9th (C) above the bass note (this is called a major 9th chord).

Riley, In C

GAM page 71   CD2 Track 3
In C
Terry Riley (b. 1935)

In Stockhausen's *Stimmung* chance events produce gradual changes of timbre without any pulse, but in Riley's *In C* a steady quaver pulse is essential for the coherence of the piece (whether or not a pianist plays repeated quaver Cs at the top of the keyboard). Where the pitches of Stockhausen's chord remain unchanged, the harmonic progression produced by performers making their way through the 53 repeating motifs of *In C* consists of a number of chords that gradually change from one to the next. Riley says that 'the most successful performances are those in which the ensemble stays within a compass of four or five patterns'. So if there were four or five performers a chord of C major coloured by a passing dissonant F♮ would emerge from the first seven motifs (enlivened by seven different rhythmic patterns).

Motifs 1–53 are numbered in *GAM*.

Motifs 8–13 make a chord of G⁷ without its 5th (D) coloured by the tonic note in motif 12. But this new chord would only emerge gradually as the performers entered bar 8 and beyond one by one. Next a series of 15 motifs outline a chord of E minor coloured by C, F♯ and A (all of them diatonic in the key of E minor). Then C major (motifs 29 and 30) and G⁷ (motifs 31–34) return before motif 35 is heard for the first time.

This motif brings about a harmonic climax because it contains F♮ and F♯, and B♮ and B♭. These pairs of pitches are as close to the seventh and eleventh harmonic of a harmonic series on C as you can get on a piano. (The seventh harmonic is 'in the crack' between B♭ and B♮, and the eleventh is similarly situated between F♯ and F♮.) It is no accident that all other pitch classes of *In C* correspond with one or more of the other ten harmonics shown here.

Brass players will recognise this as the series of pitches that can (in theory at least) be played without using valves or slide (though transposed to different pitch levels for instruments not 'in C'). In fact harmonics like these are present to a greater or lesser extent whenever a sound of definite pitch is played or sung. You cannot avoid harmonics other than by artificial electronic means, so this piece makes audible the minimal pitches that we unwittingly hear every time we listen to the note C. Of course every performance will be unique, but in all but a freak performance the effect from motif 31 to motif 41 will be of a shimmering dominant-7th chord decorated with glinting chromatic harmonics.

Reich, Clapping Music

Steve Reich took part in the first performance of Riley's *In C* and was clearly influenced by the effect of gradually changing textures, rhythms and harmony brought about by repetition and sequential change of small motifs. Out of this grew Reich's technique of phase shifting described in the notes in *GAM* on *Clapping Music* (1972). This is music stripped of every element apart from a single rhythmic motif repeated 156 times. The only variety is provided by Clap 2 moving the motif one quaver forward after each bar has been repeated 12 times while Clap 1 ruthlessly maintains precisely the same rhythm in every bar. The two parts are most out of phase in bar 7. While listening to *Clapping Music* see how the group of three quavers beamed together advance to the left at each phase change in bars 8–12 until the cycle is complete and the two clappers come back into phase with each other in bar 13.

GAM page 73   CD2 Track 4
Clapping Music
Steve Reich (b. 1936)

Reich's rhythmic effects are as hypnotic as Riley's melodic and harmonic effects, and their pioneering work is now evident, not only in the concert hall, but in many film and television scores.

Other minimalist composers

Philip Glass (b. 1937) has written several operas including *Satyagraha* (1980), which is about Gandhi, and *Akhnaten* (1983), which is about a heretical Egyptian pharaoh. Reflecting an awareness of pop music, Glass has written specifying amplification and electronic keyboards; a group of his songs was recorded by rock singer Linda Ronstadt. The string septet *Shaker Loops* (1978) and *Short Ride in a Fast Machine* (1986) are the two most famous shorter works by John Adams (b. 1947). Like Glass he has also written successful operas: *Nixon in China* (1987) and *The Death of Klinghoffer* (1989/1981). Both attracted attention for their choice of subjects from recent historical events.

Some composers have been nicknamed 'holy minimalists'. British composer John Tavener (b. 1944) and Estonian Arvo Pärt (b. 1935) have both written sacred music which uses simple materials and procedures to striking effect.

Test yourself on minimalism

Name four characteristics of minimalist music.

....

....

....

....

Performing and composing

In C is very suitable for performing in class, although you may prefer to compress the time span and use only a limited number of bars. It also makes a good model for composition. For pianists, try Tomasz Sikorski's *Diaphony for Two Pianos* (PWM 7116), an easy minimalist piece.

Clapping Music is another piece suitable for performing in class. Experiment with different types of clapping – very quiet tapping can be effective. This piece also makes a good model for composition. Why not think about an exercise based around phased football-chant rhythms?

Electronic music

A great many technological advances have occurred in the electronic art music industry. These include the invention of the tape recorder, the synthesiser and the development of processes like sampling and looping. Some of these are mentioned below, but you may find it helpful in addition to read the section on club dance remix (page 79), as this is an important example of popular electronic music.

Bedford, The Song of the White Horse: 'The Blowing Stone'

'The Blowing Stone' from *The Song of the White Horse* (1977) by David Bedford combines recorded sound with synthesised sound and live musical instruments. The real sound of the blowing stone is copied and transformed by the synthesiser and then by the brass instruments. In order to mimic the harsh siren-like effect of the blowing stone, the brass instruments play quarter-tone notes (for example the horn plays a pitch halfway between C and C♯). The notes are written close together, which creates a note 'cluster'.

An echo unit is used to produce rapid repetitions of the fanfare-like motifs that begin in bar 4, each time falling away as if the sounds are being produced in a vast closed space. If you look at the chords in bar 6 you will see that their special sound is created by combining major and minor 3rds. A dialogue (conversation) is created between the group of horn and trombones, and the trumpets. The effect of the sounds gradually getting higher in pitch and closer together is very exciting.

A helpful book covering the development and techniques of music technology is *A Student's Guide to AS and A2 Music Technology*, Cole, Collyer, Howard, Hunt and Murphy, Rhinegold Publishing, 2001.

A useful website is that of the Sonic Arts Network, the national association in the UK for electronic music at www.sonicarts network.org. A website for recent electronic music is at www.digital-music-archives.com.

> *GAM page 86*   CD2 Track 1
> *The Song of the White Horse*:
> 'The Blowing Stone'
> David Bedford (b. 1937)

The blowing stone is a large stone that creates a siren-like sound when the wind blows through it. A tape recording of this is used in this composition.

The echo unit is gradually turned up to create feedback. The original sound of the blowing stone is repeated. The tape, electronic and brass sounds fade away and are replaced by a very quiet and calm chord of G minor played on the lowest string instruments of the orchestra (cellos and double basses). Note that they play without vibrato (non vib.), and with mutes (con sord.) to create an eerie sound.

Feedback means a sort of howling sound caused by the signal continually looping round the amplifier.

Electronic composition

Although magnetic tape had been in use in the film and recording industries since the 1940s it was not until the 1950s that this technology became widely available and composers started writing music intended for tape performance, rather than performance by a live player.

Much pioneering work was carried out by the French composer Pierre Schaeffer who, in Paris in 1948, developed a style known as *musique concrète*, meaning 'music based on everyday sounds'. Schaeffer recorded the sounds of instruments, toys, whistles and speech and transformed them by playing the tape backwards, slowing it down and speeding it up, cutting and splicing sections and creating tape loops. Schaeffer also experimented with dubbing techniques – recording from one machine to another to build up thick textures. These techniques, which would have involved hours of painstaking work in the studio, are now extremely easy to produce using today's computerised digital technology. It is worth remembering that although most of them can now be produced with the click of a mouse button they are essentially the same as those developed by Schaeffer in the 1950s.

A tape loop is formed when a length of tape is joined end on end so that it runs continuously through the recorder, repeating the sound.

Two very influential composers in electronic composition are (once again) Cage and Stockhausen. Cage's *Imaginary Landscapes*, a series of pieces begun in 1939, explore chance sounds using record decks (allowing the needle to start anywhere on the disc) and short-wave radio sets (tuned to whatever randomly-found station was strongest). *HPSCHD* is an ambitious multimedia work consisting of a slideshow, seven harpsichord solos (six produced using computer programs and a seventh produced acoustically), plus acoustically transformed fragments of Mozart, Beethoven, Schumann and Chopin, and sounds generated by a computer program and recorded on to 51 audio tapes. A performance lasts about four hours and key decisions are made by the performers themselves within certain guidelines.

Maelstrom Percussion Ensemble's recording of *Imaginary Landscapes* is available on *Hat Now Series ARTCD6179*.

A recording of *HPSCHD* is available on *The Frivolous Harpsichord, Ondine ODE8912*.

Stockhausen's *Kontakte* (1960) broke new ground in combining live instruments and tape, and is widely considered to be a classic in the electronic repertoire. Percussion instruments are divided into three groups (metal, wood and membrane) and their tone colours are subjected to transformations over time as they play against prerecorded material and material generated during the actual performance. The transformations give rise to a form described by the composer as 'moment form': a process so long and drawn-out that the piece itself is merely a 'moment', the listener experiencing only a part of it as if entering and leaving a continuous film show. Stockhausen further pursued his interest in percussion and electronics in *Mikrophonie 1* (1964). This is composed for

A CD of *Kontakte* is available on *Wergo 6009*.

A CD of *Mikrophonie 1* is available on *Sony S2K 53346*.

tam-tam (gong) played live but with a variety of microphones attached so that the sounds are relayed to technicians who modify the timbre of the instrument.

We have already seen that *musique concrète* concerns the transformation of recordings of ordinary sounds. This technique plays an important part in Harrison Birtwistle's *Chronometer* (1971) which is based on the sound of clocks of all shapes and sizes set against the ostinato tick of Big Ben and the chimes of Wells Cathedral. Birtwistle used a computer to analyse the tick of Big Ben and exaggerate its small fluctuations in rhythm so that it sounds like a background heartbeat.

An extract from *Chronometer* is included in *SM*.

MIDI

The commercial development of the **synthesiser** in the 1960s and 1970s led in 1983 to the creation of **MIDI** (Musical Instruments Digital Interface). This provides a common standard to allow music-technology devices (and computers) to operate together. A **sequencer**, which these days usually takes the form of computer software, can store performance data, in much the same way that a word processor stores text. When connected to a synthesiser or **sampler** via a MIDI cable, a sequencer can act as a mechanical performer, playing the samples and electronic instruments or controlling electronic processes. It can also be used to assemble and edit compositions, displaying musical material in the form of tracks on the computer screen. While sequenced music has tended to remain the province of popular music in the preparation of backing tracks and the composition of club dance music, many composers employ sequencing as a compositional tool.

Wishart, Vox 5

> *GAM page 89*   CD2 Track 12
> *Vox 5*
> Trevor Wishart

Many electronic pieces (especially in the pop world) feature nothing but electronic instruments – no conventional instruments at all. Trevor Wishart's *Vox 5* (1986) is a work that requires the sophisticated manipulation of sound using computer technology. The piece is best understood as the electronic 'voice' of the Hindu god Shiva, who could transform himself into animals, birds and insects. Each section is a cycle of creation, transformation and destruction (including the destruction of the rain forest) and the piece includes some breathtakingly vivid moments, such as the transformation of voices into thunder, wind and swarms of bees using samples and computer manipulations.

The idea of transformation of sound is very important in this piece. There are no fixed pitches and there is no regular pulse. Instead there is a collage of natural sounds. The composer's skill is in his control of this collage.

The term to 'ululate', used in this score, means to howl, wail, or give a prolonged cry of joy. 'Panning' refers to sound travelling from one speaker to another.

The opening consists of the sounds of wind and crows. The long fade in creates the effect of a crescendo as the texture thickens. The vocal ululation is marked by extreme panning from left to right of the sound field.

At 1' 58" the sound of crowds creates a sense of space and chaos. The sudden change to the closed-in electronic sound that follows is very dramatic and is an important technique in this piece. So is the transformation of timbre, such as that from voice to bees to voice. At 3' 03" the rhythmic effect of the voices makes it sound as though they are speaking a language, but nothing can be understood. Between 3' 10" and 3' 52" the composer writes 'ingressive screech' on the score. This probably refers to the transformation of the crowd's voices into a low drone.

'Ingressive' means literally 'going in'.

Sound installation

A sound installation is an electronic-music art form which has emerged in recent years. It usually consists of background music relayed through loudspeakers and is normally found in art galleries, exhibitions and other public places. There may be an element of performance or the installation may be related in some way to a video, moving sculpture or dancer with which the music, controlled by computer, interacts. One of the first visual artists to include sound in his exhibitions was the American Jonathon Borofsky. Many composers working at the more experimental end of club dance music and ambient music, such as Aphex Twin, Orbital and Brian Eno, have been associated with installations.

Bricheno, Hyde Park

Like *Vox 5*, *Hyde Park* by Toby Bricheno is intended to be heard as a recorded rather than a live performance.

GAM page 90	CD2 Track 13
Hyde Park	
Toby Bricheno	

The music begins with high and low drones on the note D. Listen to the strange notes created by the ebow at 30". The effect of the melody that begins at 0' 40" is modal in that the melody is based on F♮ and G, not F♯. The ebow melody from 1' 41" contains an E♭ which is part of the G-minor scale. At 2' 34" the G5 chord is heard, and after that the music from 0' 40" to 1' 08" is played again, this time in reverse order. *Hyde Park* closes on G and D.

An ebow is a device held against the guitar string to create a long sustain effect.

Test yourself on electronic music

1. What is a tape loop? ....
    ....
    ....

2. What is a sampler? ....
    ....
    ....

3. Why was the invention of MIDI important? ....
    ....
    ....

4. What is meant by *musique concrète*? ....
    ....

5. *Hyde Park* makes extensive use of panning. What does this term mean? ....
    ....

6. Which of the following terms means the same as the mirror technique used by Bricheno in *Hyde Park*?

    Inversion   Retrograde   Sequence   Cadence   Modulation

7. Why do you think the use of this mirror technique is particularly appropriate in music designed for a photography exhibition?..

....

....

8. (a) Note down one dramatic sound transformation that occurs in *Vox 5* ....

....

(b) List the natural sounds that you can hear in *Vox 5*.

....

....

(c) Identify one sound that transforms into another in *Vox 5*. How long does the process take?.........................

....

....

Performing and composing

There are two recent CDs that you might find helpful to listen to. *State of the Nation 2001* features ten new works by young British composers. The music ranges from pieces for tape and prepared piano to works for full ensemble (NMC D078). *The Hoxton Thirteen* features new works by 13 even younger composers (NMC D076).

Compose a piece of electronic music for the opening of your school's new science block. It should be about two minutes in length and use at least three tracks.

Firstly you must decide on your sound sources. If you have suitable equipment available you could use the techniques of *musique concrète* and record appropriate live sounds – such as the noise of pneumatic drills to represent the construction of the building, and sounds that reflect science teaching, such as test tubes bubbling, the tone of a sine-wave generator or even the recording of the school bell. These could either be arranged as a collage, using a multi-track tape recorder, or they could be recorded as samples which you can later manipulate with a sequencer.

If you don't have suitable recording equipment for this approach, investigate the more unusual sounds on your synthesiser, such as 'sci-fi', 'sawtooth', 'sweep', 'crystal' and 'blown bottle'.

Once you have assembled your basic sounds, begin the process of layering, looping and manipulating them to create your composition. Try to create your own underlying beat (rather than just using a preset pattern such as 'disco' or ' bossa nova'). Finally, try adding a slow-moving melody on synthesiser to the texture you have created – again, look for a suitable 'sci-fi' sound, and experiment with effects such as lots of glissando between notes and perhaps some echo.

When you have finished, transfer your finished work to cassette tape, CD or mini-disc and then prepare a written commentary of the type needed for GCSE submission.

It might also be worth thinking about how the piece could be developed further. Why not compose an additional part for your school choir, which could sing alongside your electronic composition?

Popular song in context

12-bar blues

Origins of the blues

The origins of the blues can be traced to the music of Africa. During the 18th and 19th centuries Africans were forcibly transported from Africa to America to work as slaves and it is no wonder that, given the arduous lives they led, they should express sorrow and grief in their music. Their songs were not written down but were learnt by ear. This is known as an oral tradition – in other words, songs were distributed by word of mouth – and it is a feature of many types of folk music from around the world. In the southern part of the USA the songs and techniques of traditional African music interacted with the folk music of British settlers in the region, and gradually started to adopt some of its features (particularly in the use of harmony and instruments).

Folk means 'of the people'.

The songs were often about the misery of conditions the slaves had to live in under their white owners. Hence the expression 'singing the blues', meaning to sing a sad or miserable tale of woe. When they were not working, the slaves often made simple instruments to accompany their songs.

Many slaves were converted to Christianity, and another interaction, this time between European hymn tunes and African music, led to the creation of the spiritual – religious songs that once again were often on the subject of oppression.

In 1865, with the end of the Civil War, slavery ceased in the USA and African-Americans started to form bands of musicians. By the 1920s the invention of recording had enabled their music, including jazz and the blues, to become known throughout the western world. The subsequent popularisation of the blues, and the 12-bar blues chord sequence, had a far-reaching influence on the development of jazz and rock music throughout the rest of the 20th century.

Features of the blues style

Call and response

Many early blues songs contained elements found in African music, such as the use of call and response. This is where a lead singer sings phrases that are each responded to by other performers.

Blue notes

The origin of blue notes can be traced to traditional African singing, in which certain pitches are sung a little flat (not always by as much as a full semitone). Sometimes these pitches were approached by a glide into the note (a technique we now call pitch bending) to give expressive effect to the words. The notes that were sung flat were usually the third and seventh degrees of the scale. These became the standard blue notes in jazz music.

A blues scale is a scale that features the blue (or flat) 3rd and 7th, and sometimes the flat 5th as well. It can occur in various forms, of which two of the more common are C–E♭–F–G–B♭ (also known as the minor pentatonic scale) and C–E♭–F–G♭–G♮–B♭ (see *right*). In jazz the blues scale is often treated as a major scale to which is added the flat 3rd, 5th and 7th, giving the more complex pattern C–D–E♭–E♮–F–G♭–G♮–A–B♭–B♮.

Harmony Early blues songs were often unaccompanied. If an instrument (usually the guitar or banjo) was used, it either played in alternation with the voice (call and response again), or it simply played decorated versions of chord I throughout. By the 1920s a more elaborate harmonic progression had evolved. A 12-bar pattern, with one primary chord per bar, was repeated, often in the following order:

I   I   I   I   IV   IV   I   I   V   IV   I   I

The frequent use of the tonic chord, plus the prominent use of chord IV, which includes the tonic note, reveals the origins of this pattern in the old one-chord style of accompaniment.

Do you also notice the way the pattern differs from western classical (and early popular) styles? Instead of being eight or 16 bars long it is 12 bars long, and it also lacks the perfect cadence patterns (V–I) that are so characteristic of western tonal music.

12-bar blues

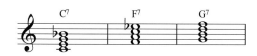

The 12-bar chord pattern of the blues has formed the basis of many types of pop music and jazz in the 20th century. There are many versions of the basic chord pattern, including some extended to 16 bars. One of the most common variants is to add a minor 7th to some or all of the chords. In the key of C major this would mean using C^7, F^7 and G^7, see *left*.

Words (lyrics)

This chord sequence, using three sets of four bars, proved to work well with the typical blues lyrics that were made up of three lines:

> Now when your best friend's quit you and you ain't done nothing wrong
> Now when your best friend's quit you and you ain't done nothing wrong
> You weep and you worry; Oh your life it won't last long.

Often, the verses are structured with the same words in lines 1 and 2. These words are important – the raw emotional lyrics relate to the innermost feelings, fears and hopes of the African Americans. Life was extremely arduous for them and music provided some release from their bitter anguish and struggle.

Rhythmic features

Swung/jazz quavers Rhythm is one of the most important features in the blues. The complex rhythms of African music gradually became simplified as European music started to influence African-American folk music in the USA, but the unequal division of the beat into long-short patterns remained a prominent feature.

This rhythmic feature was later taken up by jazz bands of the swing era, hence the term '**swung quavers**' (or 'jazz quavers'). In the music they are notated as even quavers, whereas in performance they are played more like triplets:

Written   Played

Another rhythmic legacy from Africa is syncopation, in which accents are placed on weak beats of the bars. This creates an offbeat or syncopated rhythm, as in this phrase from the blues standard, *Frankie and Johnny*, in which several beats are anticipated by the use of syncopation (marked *):

Syncopation

The original sound track of *Frankie and Johnny* is available from Curb Records, CRB 775342.

Swore to be true_ to each o - ther,   true as the skies a - bove,

Don't forget that in a blues performance the syncopation is modified by the swung rhythms mentioned above, giving an easier swing than this notation might suggest – try singing it in a relaxed rhythmic style that best fits the words.

A riff is a short repeated pattern, often used in the accompaniment. The bass part of a modern 12-bar blues will sometimes consist of a riff which is transposed as necessary to fit the chord pattern. In the bass-guitar part of *I know you lied* (see page 74) you will find the following riff:

Riff

WPA Blues

WPA Blues includes many of the features of the blues described earlier. The key is A major and the 12-bar chord pattern heard in verse 1 is:

GAM page 92	CD3 Track 1
WPA Blues	
Casey Bill Weldon	

Bar:	1	2	3	4	5	6	7	8	9	10	11	12
Chord:	A	A	A	A^7	D^7	D^7	A	A	E	E	A	A
Symbol:	I	I	I	I^7	IV^7	IV^7	I	I	V	V	I	I

The use of chord V (instead of IV) in bar 10 is a very common variant of the basic pattern. The chord of D^7 in bars 5 and 6 consists of the notes D–F♯–A–C♮.

Notice that the chord pattern is extended to 16 bars in the other verses by starting with an additional four bars of tonic chord. Listen to the use of blue notes in the melody. The recording was made in 1936 – you should be able to spot that this is an early recording from the restricted frequency range, which has little brightness and no depth to the bass notes, and the absence of stereo, which means there is no clear separation between the performers.

Many of the 12-bar-blues standard rhythmic conventions appear in this piece, such as swung quavers and syncopation. Look at the opening melody printed in *GAM* and see if you can spot two examples of syncopation. The lyrics too follow the blues theme of hardship and poverty. In this case, the song is about the Works Progress

Administration (or WPA), a scheme set up by President Roosevelt to help create jobs for the unemployed. However if you read (or listen) to the story in the lyrics, you will see that this scheme did not benefit the man at all – in fact he loses out.

I know you lied

GAM page 94   CD3 Track 2
I know you lied
Recorded by Bill Thomas

I know you lied is a 12-bar-blues composition recorded in 2001. The key signature of D♭ major makes the piece look complicated, but it is based on eight repetitions of the standard 12-bar blues chord pattern (with an added 7th on every chord):

I^7 I^7 I^7 I^7 IV^7 IV^7 I^7 I^7 V^7 IV^7 I^7 I^7

A lead-sheet is a type of score that shows just the main melody, lyrics and chord symbols.

In some verses the second chord of this pattern is changed to IV^7 (eg the chord G♭^{7} in bars 14 and 26). Such 'chord substitutions' are common in both the blues and jazz. The bass guitar part, printed after the lead-sheet in *GAM*, uses a two-bar riff, adapted to the various chord changes. The symbols at bars 37, 73 and 85 indicate 12-bar rests for the singer. At these points there are guitar breaks in which the guitarist provides impressive improvisations on the 12-bar chord pattern. The introduction also uses this pattern and the coda is based on repetitions of the last four bars of the pattern.

Note the use of modern amplified instruments (electric guitar and bass guitar) in this recording. The rhythms are mainly straight, not swung, and the drum kit takes on the important role of maintaining the beat. All of these features help make this blues sound much more modern than *WPA Blues*, recorded in 1936.

Test yourself on the blues

1. What is meant by 'call and response'?.................................
    ....

2. What are the two most common blue notes in the 'blues scale'?
    ....

3. Which of the following examples best represents the way that swung quavers are played?

    (a)

    (b)

    (c)

    (d)

4. Name the instruments that you can hear playing in *WPA Blues*.

    ....
    ....

Composing and performing

Try writing a piece in the form of the 12-bar blues (using chords I,

IV and V) that gives you the opportunity to vent your grievances about your miserable life at school: all that work, too much homework, not enough free time. Now's your chance to get your own back!

When you write your piece you must do the following:

✦ Write out your chosen 12-bar-blues chord pattern. Remember that this is not a strict cast-in-stone pattern. So you may want to subtly change a chord or two. For instance, try making chord IV minor (that would be a chord of F minor in the key of C). Or you might even try the whole 12-bar sequence in a minor key by making chord I minor as well.

An example of a different version of the 12-bar-blues sequence is the pattern in *West End Blues* by Louis Armstrong:

Bar	1	2	3	4	5	6	7	8	9	10	11	12
Chord	I	I	I	I^7	IV	IV	I	I	V^7	V^7	I	I

✦ Decide on the instrumentation, for example female voice, piano, string-bass and drums.

✦ You could use the preset chord patterns on a keyboard to provide the 12-bar blues sequence if you wish.

✦ Write some words in the style of a blues lyric, using a subject such as *Homework Blues*; *Monday Morning School Blues*; *Double Maths Blues* and so on. Remember that the verse structure is usually made up of three lines, with the same words for lines one and two. Also ensure that the words will fit the metre of the 12 bars.

✦ Compose your melody remembering to use blue notes. Plenty of falling 3rds (especially minor 3rds) will help create the right sense of style. Also use some syncopation and swung quavers.

✦ Turn the bare chord scheme into a simple, but rhythmically interesting accompaniment pattern. Refer to the 'Before You Start' chapter if you are unsure about the chords (I, IV and V). Your teacher will also be able to advise you on this matter.

✦ Try to incorporate a bass riff to provide stability to your structure.

✦ Once you have the basic structure in place, consider adding an introduction (maybe without chords) and also some solo instrumental breaks. Usually these would have been improvised on the spot, but you will need to notate them. Perhaps round the piece off with a short four bar coda over the tonic chord.

Twelve-bar-blues pieces are ideal for ensemble performances. If you are brave, you might wish to improvise your own solo breaks in between the verses. This will need to be agreed with the members of your group.

Reggae

Reggae originated in the island of Jamaica in the West Indies. The country was originally settled by the Spanish (and later taken over by the British) who imported slaves from Africa. As with the blues and jazz in America, Jamaican folk music developed from an interaction between the musical traditions of Africa and Europe – in this case, specifically Spanish traditions that were maintained

When different musical traditions interact with one another the result is often the creation of new and exciting styles – we will explore this topic more in the section on salsa starting on page 101.

and developed throughout Latin America and the Caribbean islands.

Roots of reggae

In the first half of the 20th century one of the most popular types of Jamaican music was mento. Closely related to the rumba from the nearby island of Cuba (which we mention on page 102), it features the syncopation that is so characteristic of much African-influenced music. If you have ever sung the Jamaican song *Mango Walk*, you will have an idea of the style of mento:

Mento was sometimes called 'Jamaican Rumba' in Europe – a well-known piece with this title, based on the above song, was written by Arthur Benjamin in 1938. Mento was accompanied by such instruments as the guitar, banjo, bamboo flute and bongo drums.

By the 1960s Jamaican musicians were becoming influenced by American music heard on the radio, particularly rhythm and blues and big-band jazz. This resulted in a new style called ska. It combined the memorable melodies of mento with swung rhythms and it used instruments such as trumpets, saxophones, electric guitars and electric organs. An early ska song that (most unusually) reached number two in the UK charts in 1964 was 'My Boy Lollipop' sung by the Jamaican-born Millie Small:

The clipped style, with frequent rests in the vocal part and staccato interjections from trumpets, is characteristic of ska, as are the swung rhythms (shown by the triplet brackets) and the walking bass in crotchets. But the most important element is the accent of the off-beats (beats 2 and 4) by the snare drum. This accent pattern (known as a backbeat) later became the hallmark of reggae.

By 1966 ska itself was changing. Influenced by American soul and gospel music, the bass became heavier and more dominant, and the tempo became slower. The music focused on short repeated patterns based on a limited number of chords, although the prominent backbeat of ska was retained. The result was known as rock steady and its stars included Jimmy Cliff and Desmond Dekker. Their songs were often about poverty and the music was played very loudly through sound systems – since not many people could afford record players this became a sort of free communal music.

In 1969 Desmond Dekker had a number one hit in the UK with his song *The Israelites*. His 1970 recording of Jimmy Cliff's rock-steady song *You can get it if you really want* is included in *NAM*.

Reggae itself appeared in the late 1960s. Like ska and rock steady, it makes use of swung rhythms and a prominent backbeat, but it has a slower tempo than rock steady – you will probably find yourself tapping eight quavers (rather than four crotchets) to the bar in both of the reggae pieces in *GAM*. The role of the bass became even more important, and the slower speed allowed the use of intricate, syncopated bass patterns which are treated as riffs. These patterns usually avoid important beats, such as the first beat of the bar. Most of the other parts are also based on riffs, including the clipped, off-beat guitar chords and the repeated hook motifs that are often played on an electric organ.

Make sure that you can identify all of these features in both of the reggae pieces in *GAM*. Notice how the drummer introduces both pieces and then maintains eight steady quavers per bar on the hi-hat cymbal in addition to emphasising the backbeats on both bass drum and snare drum. Notice too how chordal instruments, such as the guitar, electric organ and/or piano, play mainly on off-beats in both songs, contributing to the syncopated effect. The constantly repeating chord pattern in both numbers adds to the hypnotic effect of the repeating riffs.

Freedom Fighters

In *Freedom Fighters* the vocal melody is also constructed from riffs, which are adapted to fit the words. It is thought that the name 'reggae' comes from the word 'regular', referring to the regularity of its repeated musical patterns.

Reggae began during a long period of social unrest that followed Jamaica's independence from Britain in 1964. Disillusioned that their own government were unable to solve the severe economic problems, many Jamaicans turned to Rastafarianism – the songs of Bob Marley and Peter Tosh, two of reggae's most famous stars, are steeped in Rastafarian beliefs and carry strong political messages.

Rastafarians and rude boys

Rastafarianism began as an outlaw religious group based in Jamaica. Rastas believe that God took earthly form in the person of Ras Tafari Makonnen, who was proclaimed Emperor Haile Selassie of Ethiopia (in Africa) in 1930, and who visited Jamaica in 1966. They look to the time when one day black people will return to the 'promised land', the country of Ethiopia. It is through their performance of reggae music that they voice their beliefs in peace, love and brotherhood. The struggle against the corrupt western civilisation (called 'Babylon') is also a political feature in the words of their reggae songs. The hypnotic trancelike nature of their music has been linked to the taking of ganja (the drug cannabis – 'a holy herb') as part of their religious ritual. There are also references to this in the lyrics of some songs.

Reggae was also the music of the 'rude boys', street criminals based in Kingston, Jamaica. Many of the recordings were promoted by DJs who would often talk over the music, using it rather like a backing track. This became known as dubbing. The practice of dubbing is also important in later musical styles such as rap. The active role of

The subject of reggae songs can be summarised as:	
Poverty	the poverty of parts of Jamaica
Politics	the struggle against western civilisation
Religion	worship of Jah Rastafari
Peace, love and brotherhood	a common theme of 1960s pop

Why Babylon? Because of the Babylonian captivity suffered by part of the Israelite nation: the story is in the book of Ezekiel in the Old Testament.

the DJ in Britain and America also developed considerably around this time. Consider, for example, the important role of the DJ in the disco music of the 1970s and 1980s.

Real Rock

Riddim

Real Rock is an example of 'riddim'. The word is Jamaican for rhythm but it implies more than that. It is a type of pattern that modern pop musicians would call a 'groove', where the combination of drums and bass is so memorable that it colours the whole song. Riddims from existing pieces are often borrowed and reused to form the basis of new compositions. The one in *Real Rock* first appeared in recordings made in the legendary Studio One in Kingston, Jamaica in the late 1960s and early 1970s.

Here is a comparison of the two reggae pieces in *GAM*, the first is vocal with instrumental accompaniment, and the second is just instrumental:

GAM page 96   CD3 Track 3
Freedom Fighters
Recorded by Delroy Washington

GAM page 98   CD3 Track 4
Real Rock
Recorded by Sound Dimension

Clavinet is not a misprint for 'clarinet': it is a five-octave electric keyboard.

	Freedom Fighters	**Real Rock**
Instrumentation	Vocals (melody), drums, bass guitar, clavinet, organ, guitar	Trombone (melody), drums, bass guitar, organ, piano, guitar
Characteristics	Both are simple and repetitive; both use blue notes and syncopation	
Structure	Intro, then verse-chorus	Intro, then repeated section with variation
Chords	Three chords in a four-bar pattern	Two chords in a one-bar pattern
Time signature	Both in common quadruple time ($\frac{4}{4}$) with swung semiquavers	
Accompaniment	Snare and bass drum play on beats 2 and 4	Snare and bass drum play on beats 2 and 4
	Guitar plays off-beat quavers	Guitar and piano play off-beat quavers
	Bass guitar plays repeated four-bar riff	Bass guitar plays repeated one-bar riff
	Organ plays rapidly repeated chords	Organ plays a three-note hook
	Clavinet plays a three-note hook	

Influences of the reggae style in Britain

Reggae did not become widely known in Britain until Eric Clapton recorded a cover version of Bob Marley's *I Shot the Sheriff* in 1974. Within a few years groups such as the Clash, the Police and Madness were drawing on ideas from reggae – the music of Sting (formerly in the Police) has sometimes been described as 'white reggae'. More recent influences can be detected in the music of ragga artists such as Shaggy.

Ragga is a style of reggae music that also borrows influences from from hip hop and drum 'n' bass.

? Test yourself on reggae

1. What are the main differences between ska, rock steady and reggae?...
....
....
....

2. Which beats of the bar are stressed in reggae? ....

3. In *Freedom Fighters* by Delroy Washington:

   (a) Name two features of the melody line.

   ....

   ....

   (b) Which rhythms are swung in this piece: quavers or semiquavers? ....

4. In *Real Rock* from Sound Dimension.

   (a) Name the instrument playing the tune ....

   (b) How is this piece typical of the reggae style? Mention two features. ....

   ....

Performing and composing

If you aren't attracted by any of the subjects listed on page 77, write an instrumental dance piece in a reggae style for a colourful carnival procession.

Your own composition is one possibility for performance. Another idea might be to get hold of the sheet music of a well-known reggae number, like Bob Marley's *I Shot the Sheriff* or *Jammin'* and arrange the piece for an ensemble to play.

When you have learnt the tune, add three accompaniment parts:

◆ the bass riff

◆ continuous quavers played on cymbals (or other percussion)

◆ strong chords on beats 2 and 4 played by keyboard or guitar.

When you are happy with the arrangement, give a performance.

I Shot the Sheriff and other Bob Marley songs can be found in the compilation book **Bob Marley: Songs of Freedom**, *Music Sales*, AM 91060.

Club dance remix

In club dance remix samples of original recordings from various artists are rearranged through the use of technology. Various forms of club music originated from the 1980s rave culture, and styles such as house and techno. Remixing has been used as a tool to bring songs and styles from non-club culture (such as pop or rock) into dance clubs. Nowadays the music relies strongly on advanced music-technology resources and is closely allied with the popularity of dance culture.

Origins

Since the disco phenomenon of the 1970s, club-dance music has become increasingly popular. Discos featured powerful sound systems and multi-coloured flashing lighting effects. The main feature in all the music was a fast, driving rhythm. In the 1980s disco music used advanced synthesisers and sampled music. Other forms of disco music evolved, including acid-house music. The rave-culture scene of the 1980s catered for mass gatherings, often held illegally in disused buildings. The description 'acid house', despite the common opinion that it is an overt reference to drug taking, was in fact to do with the process of sampling music. ('Acid burning' was Chicago slang for sampling.) Raves would feature music generated by synthesisers, drum machines and heavily sampled music. Throughout the 1980s and 1990s, techno-dance styles developed apace. This led to spin-off dance styles including garage, trance, jungle and drum 'n' bass.

Technology

Music technology has under-pinned the rise of a modern dance culture: to understand club dance remix, you need to understand the technology. Over recent years, it has become highly sophisticated, affordable and widespread. This has made it possible for ordinary people to produce high-quality music without the need to seek contracts with recording companies or hire expensive studios. It is one of the reasons for the recent explosion of musical styles. The internet has made it possible to distribute and exchange tracks as computer-files, thus bypassing the commercial market that often dictated tastes in pop music throughout much of the last century. The following devices are central to the process of creating remixes.

Sampler
Turn back to page 68 for MIDI.

A sampler can record and process short extracts from existing recordings. The samples are stored in digital format and a MIDI signal can be used to trigger their replay. A piece of club-dance music might well contain many such samples taken from a wide range of other pieces. This is a form of systematic borrowing, but it does call into question the degree of originality found in remixes. It is rather like you handing in an essay made up entirely of quotations. Although remixes cannot be viewed strictly as compositions, they do require creative processes to be employed to achieve the desired effect.

Drum machine

A drum machine is a synthesiser that enables the creation of different drum patterns and rhythms. Often these are used to generate continuous drum loops. These drum loops will be quite short, ie one, two or four bars long. Today it is more common to create a drum track on a computer-based sequencer.

The DJ

In the 1970s and 1980s the disc jockey (DJ) became an essential figure in hosting discos and operating the turntables. In more recent years, the DJ has taken an even more prominent position. From the early 1980s they have adopted the role of performance artists, able to mix their own music using the sort of technology outlined above. They are able to make live mixes using a combination of samplers and turntables, known as decks. This requires considerable skill in the synchronisation of the various tracks, without evidence of a join. The tracks must be mixed at exactly the same speed or beats per minute (bpm).

Only experienced DJs can create a stream of dance numbers that appears seamless due to a continuous beat, usually generated by a drum machine. Another common technique is called 'scratching', which involves moving a vinyl record backwards and forwards manually while it is playing, creating distortions.

Many DJs today, especially radio DJs, store and mix their music digitally on a computer.

Common elements

In a club dance remix diverse samples are mixed into one collage of sound texture. The format means that there is a series of episodes over the foundation of drums and bass.

Drum and bass

In some mixes, the drum and bass drops out for a while, making an impression when they re-enter, highlighting the extreme low frequencies and varying the texture. This is particularly effective on powerful club PA systems.

Drum loops

Drum loops are repeated rhythm patterns of varying length. Their repetitiveness can be quite hypnotic.

Breaks

Breaks are sections for a solo instrument or instruments.

Spellbound

In *GAM* there are three different mixes of *Spellbound*. These show some common procedures and techniques used in club dance remix. However if you listen to the three mixes one after the other, you will become aware that each mix is quite different from the other. The basic idea is to take an original track and change it by taking out parts, adding in new parts, changing the structure and so on to produce a reinterpretation of the original music.

GAM pages 99–102   CD3 Tracks 5–7
Spellbound
Rae and Christian
Rae and Christian remix dub
Andy Madhatter and Si Brad

The major difference between mix 1 and mix 2 is that in the first there is a recognisable song format of verses, bridges, choruses and instrumental breaks. This is not the case in the second mix, where the collage technique is used and therefore the structure is much looser. There is a series of episodes with only the briefest snatch of vocal melody from the original song. The third mix is slightly different again. While this mix retains the verse-chorus idea, several sections are used without the vocal part, for example bar 93 to the end.

Structure

In mix 1 loops are used to create the drum-and-bass tracks. These form the essential rhythmic backing of the entire song. Listen to how closely related the drum part is to the bass.

In mix 2, as has already been mentioned, the structure is looser and is built up using various collages or musical episodes. As in mix 1 there is still the firm foundation of the drum and bass providing a strong rhythmic basis to the music. Unlike mix 1, a new bass part has been composed.

Although the original vocal part is largely 'cut', the mix highlights the use of the original backing vocals. These are taken from the chorus of the song and are used as hooks.

A hook is a short repeated motif.

Not only do we have a new bass line, but many of the loops are new too. Various technological processes have been applied to create new sounds, for example a piano chord is played backwards, and digital effects are used, such as delay and distortion. As in the first mix, much use is made of syncopation in the rhythmic elements of the music. This helps to give the music an upbeat lively feeling.

The structure of mix 3 is rather more like mix 1, ie it uses a verse and chorus. Again the guitar and bass parts are similar, in this case provided by a funk guitar and piano. However in this mix the drums have been simplified and new bass lines have been added. There is also a new chord sequence to add some variety to the mix. Much use is made of looped samples in the music.

When you listen to this mix notice how these various timbres create a different sonority from that in either mix 1 or 2. Each mix is different, not only in terms of the instruments and effects used, but also in the way in which the new material is presented. It is the manipulation of the technological resources that enables musicians to create countless remixes of the same original piece.

Cosmic Interlude

GAM page 103   CD3 Track 8
Cosmic Interlude
Recorded by LTJ Bukem

The composer of *Cosmic Interlude* is Danny Williamson, the real name of its performer (LTJ Bukem).

Cosmic Interlude by LTJ Bukem is similar in many ways to the second mix of *Spellbound* in that it employs the collage technique as a means of structure. Using your knowledge of the various techniques used in club dance remix, make a short list of four techniques/effects that are used in this mix.

? Test yourself on club dance remix

1. What were the origins of club dance remix?

   ....

   ....

2. Name some of the common equipment used.

   ....

   ....

3. Explain the terms musical sample, scratching, collage, remix and drum loop. ....

   ....

   ....

   ....

   ....

4. Briefly define the role of the DJ in club dance music.

   ....

   ....

5. What is the musical function of the drum and bass part?

   ....

   ....

   ....

Composing and performing

Create an abstract piece of club dance remix using a collage technique to mix together various samples. These can be taken from music of a variety of time periods, but try to include some from the classical and popular repertoire, and organise them into a musical collage. As a starting point, draw a track diagram to plan out your intended mix. Examples of track diagrams can be found in *GAM* (pages 101–103).

Remember to log your processes carefully as this will be assessed at a later date. You will need to include at least three simultaneous tracks or varying timbres in your mix.

Obviously, the performance will only require the pressing of a start button. However it would be useful to have some feedback or appraisal from your class on the effectiveness (or lack of) of the mix. Do the features that you have intended work in the mix? For example is the sampling effective? Do the collages work?

Songs from musicals

A musical (originally 'musical play' or 'musical comedy') is a theatrical work in which music plays a central function. The music is in a popular style: as jazz and rock became dominant, so musicals were written in those styles. In addition the musical borrowed from the structures and methods of opera. As with opera, composers of musicals had to make sure the music helped to tell a dramatic story and to create convincing characters. A musical generally has orchestral or band accompaniment, and will usually include solo songs, duets, choruses and often dance numbers, usually separated by sections of spoken dialogue. Inspiration for the storylines come from various sources, drama of course, but also fiction, poetry and the Bible. Sources include Charles Dickens' *Oliver Twist*, Victor Hugo's *Les Misérables*, Shakespeare's play *Romeo and Juliet*, the poetry of T S Eliot's *Old Possum's Book of Practical Cats* and the biblical book of Exodus: can you match each of these sources to the name of a famous musical?

The American musical is sometimes called the Broadway musical – a reference to the street (Broadway) in New York where many theatres hosting these elaborate spectacles are located. In Britain the term 'West End musical' refers to London's West End, where there are also many theatres that stage musicals.

Background

The early musical comedy, as it was known, started in America and soon became an elaborate, large-scale form of entertainment. One of the first successful musicals was *Show Boat* (1927) by Jerome Kern. One of the most productive collaborations was between Richard Rodgers (music) and Oscar Hammerstein (words). Their successes included *Oklahoma!* (1943), *Carousel* (1945), *The King and I* (1951) and *The Sound of Music* (1959).

All four of these musicals were filmed.

After the list of hit musicals of the 1940s and 1950s by Rodgers and Hammerstein, the musical temporarily declined in popularity. Interest shifted to new forms of popular music, such as the Beatles' songs.

Then in the 1960s another famous partnership was formed – Andrew Lloyd Webber and Tim Rice. Their first musical was called *Joseph and the Amazing Technicolor Dreamcoat* (1968). This quickly became a resounding success, so much so that extra sections were written to create a full-scale stage production. For many years this musical has remained a favourite with schoolchildren and many staged performances have taken place.

Joseph was originally written for a school choir. *Joseph and the Amazing Technicolor Dreamcoat* is published by Novello and Co Ltd.

Lloyd Webber and Rice went on to write other hit shows, including *Jesus Christ Superstar* (1971) and *Evita* (1978). Lloyd Webber has also written *Cats* (using the poems of T S Eliot), *Starlight Express* (with lyricist Richard Stilgoe) and *Phantom of the Opera* (with lyricist Charles Hart).

West Side Story's lyricist Stephen Sondheim went on to become a famous composer of musicals in his own right.

The 1993 recording of West Side Story based on the Leicester Haymarket production of the musical is available from TER, TER 1197.

Other composers have become famous through composing only one major work, eg Lionel Bart's *Oliver!* (1960) or Claude-Michel Schönberg's *Les Misérables* (1980). However perhaps the most famous work in this genre was an American musical written in 1957 by Leonard Bernstein. It is of course *West Side Story*.

West Side Story

This work is based on Shakespeare's play *Romeo and Juliet* with the story brought up to date and set on the violent West Side of New York. In the musical Shakespeare's 'two households both alike in dignity' become two rival street gangs, the Jets and the Sharks. Romeo becomes Tony and Juliet becomes Maria. There are many other transformations, eg the masked ball of the Capulets now takes place in a shabby youth-club gymnasium, and the balcony scene is set on a rusty fire-escape of a dilapidated block of tenements.

However the central themes remain the same – both play and musical are stories of the secret love between two people who, despite the feuding of their communities, wish for a brighter future. Both stories end in tragedy.

Songs

Make sure you listen to the different *types* of song to be found in a musical. If you have a recording of *West Side Story* at your school, listen to the following suggested songs taken from the different categories below. Any other musical will do just as well. In broad terms these are as follows:

Solo (or duet) character number

This expresses the character's feelings at that particular point in the story, eg love, anxiety, anger, sadness, happiness. Solo (or duet) character numbers include:

'Maria'	Dreamy, romantic number, slow and sustained.
'Tonight' (duet)	Again, a dreamy, romantic love song between Tony and Maria.
'One hand, one heart' (duet)	Romantic ballad.
'Somewhere'	Expressive melody, tinged with sadness and grief.
'A boy like that' (duet)	An angry dialogue between Anita and Maria using speech rhythms to reflect the anger of Anita as she criticises Maria.
'I have a love'	Maria's simple statement of love for Tony sung in the context of a slow, romantic ballad.

Action song

The point of this type of song is to move the action along to the next scene. For example:

'Something's coming'	Fast, excited, restless mood.
'Tonight' (quintet)	The main characters plot the night's events as the gangs take to the streets.

Many musicals also contain chorus numbers in which either the whole cast (or a substantial section of it) sings, although in *West Side Story* most of the large ensembles are dances rather than choruses.

Despite the differences in musical style, many of these types of vocal music developed originally in opera.

Consider yourself

The musical *Oliver!* is based on the Charles Dickens novel *Oliver Twist*. Lionel Bart, the composer of the music, once summarised the central theme of the story as the search for love. Oliver yearns for his lost mother, Nancy strives for the affection of Bill Sykes and even old Fagin finds comfort in his 'family' of young pickpockets. The story tells of a boy born in a Victorian workhouse to a mother of good breeding, who sadly dies in childbirth. One mealtime, Oliver makes an audacious request for more food, and as a result, he is summarily sold off to the highest bidder. There then follows a series of adventures.

Oliver befriends the Artful Dodger and goes to live with the gang of pickpockets led by Fagin. The song 'Consider yourself' is a kind of welcome piece, as Oliver is told to consider himself 'one of the family'. The song itself is a lively and jaunty piece. It is written in B♭ major and has a 'moderate march tempo'. The $\frac{6}{8}$ metre has a two-in-a-bar feel. The four-bar introduction is almost comic and sets off the piece in a humorous mood. The melody is quite repetitive – notice that the phrase 'consider yourself' returns frequently and in addition features the use of chromatic notes to add colour and character to the music. A substantial part of the melodic part relies on this chromatic feature. Harmony is largely diatonic, but like the melody lines, there are several colourful chromatic chords, for example the diminished 7th in bar 2. The simple crotchet–quaver, crotchet–quaver rhythm of the bass part in most bars gives the music its almost skipping and dance-like rhythm. In summary, this is a bold and brassy tune, ideal for a dance sequence. Note that the song has no separate chorus as such, but is made up of four lively and dramatic verses.

Cabaret

Cabaret by John Kander and Fred Ebb opened at the Broadhurst Theatre on 20 November 1966 and ran for 1,165 performances. The musical is set in the tumultuous city of Berlin just before Hitler's rise to power. It is based on two sources, the stories of Christopher Isherwood and John Van Druten's play *I am a Camera*. The main action centres around Sally Bowles, a cabaret entertainer at the seedy Kit Kat Club and her affair with Clifford, a writer. He takes her in after she loses her job at the club and a love affair develops.

The title song 'Cabaret' is sung by Sally Bowles as part of her entertainment at the club. You will hear a drum roll followed by the MC announcing her act 'Und now, once again, Fraulein Bowles'. This famous song has a complex form and there are many changes in tempo. The melodic structure of the sections is as follows:

GAM page 104   CD 3 Track 9
'Consider yourself' from *Oliver!*
Lionel Bart

The version in *GAM* is taken from the vocal score. This is a type of score in which the orchestral parts are simplified and arranged on two staves so that they can be played on the piano. The complete vocal score of *Oliver!* is published by Lakeview Music Publishing and is also available from Music Sales.

The word 'chromatic' is actually derived from the word 'colour'.

GAM page 108   CD 3 Track 10
'Cabaret' from *Cabaret*
John Kander and Fred Ebb

In 1972 a film version was made starring Liza Minnelli as Sally, Joel Grey as the MC and Michael York as Clifford.

Intro 1–8	A 9–39	B 40–48	A 49–64	Link 65–66³	C 66⁴–97³	'Recit' 97⁴–101	A 102–132	B' 133–141	A 142–169 D♭ major

The direction 'Cakewalk' in bar 142 refers to an early ragtime style.

Apart from the introduction and last section, most of the piece is in C major, although there are many chromatic inflexions and chords that colour the music. These are obvious influences from jazz music as are the frequent use of syncopated rhythms. The orchestral accompaniment contains many colourful effects and, in addition to providing a solid chordal foundation to the melody, adds rhythmic interjections from muted brass and saxophones. In the last section, a solo trumpet is assigned an effective counter-melody to the singer's melody. Look closely at the score to observe some of the effective scoring, for example in the slow section on page 113, to the words, 'what good is sitting alone in your room?', the orchestration used is pizzicato strings, piano and banjo, playing pianissimo.

 Test yourself on musicals

1. Name the two Americans who wrote some of the most well-known musicals in the 1940s and 1950s.

   ....

2. What is the effect of modulating up a semitone in the last section of the song 'Cabaret'?

   ....

   ....

   ....

Try to look at three of the following songs:

Cats
(i)   'Skimbleshanks: The Railway Cat'
(ii) 'The Old Gumbie Cat'
(iii) 'The Rum Tum Tugger'
Oliver!
(i)   'Food Glorious Food'
(ii) 'Where is Love?'
(iii) 'Pick a Pocket or Two'
Les Misérables
(i)   'Do you hear the People Sing'
(ii) 'Castle on a Cloud'
(iii) 'Master of the House'

3. Compare and contrast three songs from *Cats*, *Oliver!* or *Les Misérables*. Use the following headings in your comparisons:

   (i)   key (major/minor)

   (ii) tempo (same or varied)

   (iii) mood and character

   (iv) rhythmic features

   (v)   structure (form)

   (vi) accompaniments.

Composing

Write a song for a musical which is based on world mythology, a folk legend or a historical event. Take one of the songs you have listened to recently as a model. Write your own song in a similar style, copying the elements you like, such as structure, length of sections and key scheme including modulations. This could be a solo, duet or chorus song. You may even use the same words, but don't copy the melody.

Performing

If you take up any of the composing suggestions, try to perform them in class. All being well this will give you some useful feedback on ways to improve your work. Your accompaniment could be just for piano for example. If you have time, you might like to sequence a more elaborate accompaniment for synthesiser or even attempt an arrangement for small band.

Remember to log any changes or alterations that you make to your music, as this will provide you with some useful material when it comes to writing up the 'Understanding the Brief'.

Remember that selections of songs from shows will only include a few of the numbers, and these will usually be heavily arranged and simplified. If you want to see how all of the songs in a musical fit together you will need at least a vocal score. These are available for most of the musicals we have mentioned.

Indian rãg

The music of the Indian subcontinent has two principal traditions, the Hindustani tradition of north India and the Carnatic tradition of south India.

Indian music in context

There are many different types of music in India today. These include classical, religious, folk and popular styles such as film music, just as we have similar categories of music in the west. However we will study north Indian classical music. This is a tradition with origins steeped in legends that proclaim that music was enjoyed by the deities (gods). The stories of these Hindu gods have been passed down through generations, and the music is viewed as having special religious and philosophical significance.

You may encounter different spellings of the terms 'rãg' (such as raga and ragam) and 'tãl' (such as tala and talam).

Musical performances take place in temples and at religious festivals. Some may last all day and night. Even today, rãg performances can last for several hours.

This form of learning is called oral tradition.

The study of music takes place without notation and is based on an intense system of listening and memorising. Master and student belong to a gharana or 'extended family' which includes actual family members and others who are 'adopted' as pupils. Gharanas are all different and have their own beliefs and musical preferences for performance style. Students add their own personal ideas and techniques to what they have already have been taught.

What is a rãg?

Melodic improvisation in Indian music is based upon a set collection of ascending and descending notes. This is called a rãg, which can be described as being somewhere in between a melody and a scale.

Quite often the ascending and descending forms of the rãg are different, and specific pitches are stressed and/or ornamented.

There are many rãgs, each with its own name, for example 'Yaman' and 'Kalyan'. Look at *The Rãg Guide: a Survey of 74 Hindustani Rãgs* (ed) Joep Bor, Nimbus Records with Rotterdam Conservatory of Music 1999.

The way that the pitches of each rãg relate to each other is important as some pitches will only be hinted at, whereas others will be embellished, and sometimes it is required that certain pitches are played slightly flat or sharp. There are also melodic phrases that are characteristic of each rãg. Each rãg has an association with a certain time of day or night, or season, resulting in particular moods or feelings being evoked, and traditionally rãgs were only played at their specified times.

To indicate a note in the upper octave, a dot is placed above the note (eg Ṡ), when an octave below a dot below is added (eg Ṣ).

In Indian music, the seven degrees (or *svaras*) are called by the syllables: *sa, ri, ga, ma, pa, dha, ni*. *Ri, ga, dha* and *ni* can all be flattened (*komal* = flat) and *ma* can be sharpened (*tivra* = sharp). *Sa* (tonic) can be on any pitch. When improvising on a rãg it is considered bad practice to sound notes that do not belong to the rãg.

What is a tāl?

The basis for rhythmic improvisation is a cycle of beats called a tāl. The tāl is divided into a fixed number of beats (*matras*). A tāl is distinguished by the number of *matras*, and by how they are grouped together. Two common tāl patterns are *rupaka*, a seven-beat cycle where the beats are grouped 3+2+2; and *teental*, a 16-beat cycle where the beats are grouped 4+4+4+4. Within this rhythmic framework, the percussionist will base their improvisations upon a predetermined pattern of strokes, or *theka*. The first beat of the cycle is called *sam*. If we look at *teental* the *theka* pattern is represented by the following syllables:

The name *tali* means 'handclap' and the rhythmic framework of the tāl is often clapped by the audience, or by the pupil's teacher.

clap				clap				wave				clap			
1	2	3	4	5	6	7	8	9	10	11	12	13	14	15	16
dha	*dhin*	*dhin*	*dha*	*dha*	*dhin*	*dhin*	*dha*	*dha*	*tin*	*tin*	*ta*	*ta*	*dhin*	*dhin*	*dha*
sam															

Each one of these syllables represents a different way of hitting the drum with the fingers. The syllables are often spoken by the drummer. The basic structure of the tāl can be represented by handclaps, which have been indicated here. A 'wave' means hitting the palm of your left hand with the back of your right hand (or the other way round if you are left handed!), and signifies a weaker beat. It is very important that the drummer and the vocal/instrumental soloist start their improvisations from the same beat, so *sam* (the first beat) is often clearly accented.

Can you see how the syllables change slightly after a 'wave'? At this point the drummer plays a slightly different pattern of finger strokes.

Performing Indian music

The size and make up of an Indian classical-music ensemble can vary, although *usually* there will be the following participants:

◆ A solo singer or an instrumentalist playing, for example, the sitar, sarod, sarangi, bansuri or shenhai. A violin often echoes the soloist's melody

◆ A drummer playing the tāl patterns. This is often played on two small drums called tabla

◆ A drone played on the tanpura. The drone is usually played on *sa* and *pa*, the first and fifth degrees of the rāg.

Instrument names are explained on page 90.

A typical rāg performance

While there will inevitably be many exceptions, a typical rāg performance will have a formal structure around which the improvisation is cast.

In the alap, the opening improvisatory section, the notes of the rāg are gradually introduced by the soloist. This section is unaccompanied (apart from the tanpura drone) and is unmetred. It can last for up to 45 minutes and is in a slow tempo.

Alap

Unmetred means 'free time'.

The improvised music becomes more structured in the jhor and it is now possible to feel a sense of metre. This section is still an improvisation on the rāg at a medium tempo.

Jhor

During the jhala the music becomes faster and more rhythmic. The improvisation further explores the notes of the rāg and various colourful techniques are employed. The section is usually taken at a fast tempo.

Jhala

| Gat/Bandish | This is the final section where a fixed composition is brought into play. It is at this point that the drummer enters. The soloist, if an instrumentalist, will play a *gat* (instrumental composition) to which improvised flourishes are often added. With the introduction of the drum(s), the rhythm takes on an important role and drummer and soloist often engage in dialoguing with each other. |

In a vocal performance, the fixed composition is called a *bandish* which is essentially a song in four clear sections – *sthayi*, *antara*, *samcari* and *abhog*.

The entire performance might last from 30 minutes to five hours – or more.

The final gat or bandish is interspersed with sections of rãg improvisation. The performance will typically end with a dramatic flourish of virtuoso display.

Indian instruments

Voice The human voice is considered to be of particular significance in Indian classical music as it is believed that by singing, you are directly communicating with God. The importance of the voice is highlighted by the fact that all other melody instruments try and recreate the timbre of the human voice.

Sitar

Sitar This is a long-necked plucked-string instrument with a gourd sound-box. There are six or seven main strings (two of which are drone strings) and these are plucked with a wire plectrum. There is also a set of 12 (or more) loosely-fretted sympathetic strings running beneath the main strings which vibrate 'in sympathy' when the main strings are played. This gives the instrument its characteristic, slightly distorted sound. A common playing technique is to alter the pitch of a note by pulling the string across the fret. Another technique is a microtonal slide or portamento referred to as *mind*.

Tanpura This instrument is similar in shape to the sitar, but with a smaller sound-box and a longer neck. The instrument has only four strings, each of which is tuned to the drone notes of the particular rãg being used.

Tanpura

Sarod This is smaller than the sitar and has a fretless metal fingerboard, meaning that the instrumentalist is able to slide their fingernails up and down the strings. Like the sitar it has both plucked and sympathetic strings.

Tabla

These are a set of two small drums of different sizes. Technically, the full name should be *tabla-baya* as the *tabla* is the smaller drum and the *baya*, the larger one. The drum heads are both made of skin, with a paste of iron filings and flour in the centre of each instrument. The *tabla* drum is made of wood, whereas the *baya* is made of metal.

Other north-Indian instruments include: *sarangi* (small, fretless, bowed-string instrument) *shenhai* (double-reed instrument a bit like an oboe); *bansuri* (bamboo flute); and *pakhawaj* (double-ended drum).

Rãg Brindabani Sarang

GAM page 123   CD3 Track 14
Rãg Brindabani Sarang

In *Rãg Brindabani Sarang* you will hear three main sections from a full rãg performance – the opening introductory *alap* followed by two *gat* sections (one slow, one fast). The *jhor* and *jhala* are omitted here. The rãg itself refers to a town called Brindaban, which has strong associations with the Hindu god Krishna.

The piece itself features the sarod, tanpura and tabla. The tabla can be heard in the *gat* sections. You will hear two tāl patterns in this piece – *dhamar* (a 14 beat cycle) and *teental* (a 16 beat cycle).

The improvisations on the sarod include three common playing techniques. First, the frequent sliding between notes. As there are no frets on the sarod, the sliding effects, called *mind*, are continuous. Second, rapid flourishes up and down in a scalic fashion is called a *tan*. Third, you will sometimes hear a repeated phrase on the tabla called a *tihai*. These are patterns that are played three times to signal that *sam* (the first beat of the tāl cycle) is approaching. The *tihai* usually ends on *sam*.

Rāg Durga

In this composition there is a vocalist, tanpura and tabla. The music is in praise of Durga, a Hindu goddess. The musical structure features an opening introductory *alap* section followed by a precomposed song. You can see the melodic outline of this piece in *GAM* and also the notes of the Durga rāg.

GAM page 122	CD3 Track 13
Rāg Durga	

The melodic outline gives a clearer indication of how the notes of the rāg will be treated in performance.

This rāg is pentatonic. The tanpura drone uses the notes *sa* and *pa* (here C and G). During the main section, you will hear the tabla playing the 16-beat tāl *teental*.

Test yourself on Indian music

1. What is a rāg? ....

2. (i) What is the main function of the tanpura? ....

   ....

   (ii) What are the tabla and what do they play? ....

   ....

4. What happens in the *alap* section of a typical performance of Indian classical music? ....

   ....

5. How would you describe the mood of Rāg Durga? Does it change or remain the same? ....

   ....

6. Outline four characteristic features of Indian music heard in Rāg Durga. Refer to the instruments, melody, rhythm and structure. ....

   ....

   ....

   ....

   ....

Performing

Try to create an *alap* (the opening improvisatory section of a rāg performance) using *hansadvani* rāg. The rāg is as follows:

We have notated this rāg as being in C major. However rāgs can start on any note, so your 'Sa' could be E, G♯, B … whichever key suits your instrument.

As the *alap* section is unmetred you will not have to worry about playing in a set number of bars or beats. Instead concentrate on the melodic aspect and explore the notes of the rāg as you improvise. Try to follow these guidelines:

✦ Rāg improvisations usually move gradually into the lower octave, slowly work their way into the middle and high octaves, and then eventually return to the middle tonic 'Sa'.

✦ Introduce each note of the rāg gradually, perhaps by putting a turn around each note (for example sa ri sa ni sa, see *left*).

✦ The note 'Pa' (here G) is second-most in importance after 'Sa', so when playing this note make sure it is prominent – maybe by making it slightly louder and longer than its preceding note.

You could get a friend to simulate a drone on a keyboard instrument, either by sounding a chord consisting of tonic-dominant-tonic or by playing these notes one after another (see *left*).

You might like to consult *World Sound Matters* by Jonathan Stock, Schott Educational (topics 19–21, Music for Vina, Nagasvaram and Pakhavaj) and *Fortissimo* by Roy Bennett, Cambridge University Press, ISBN 0-521-569-23-0 (text) ISBN-9-521-569-25-7 (set of four compact discs) (look at two pieces on pages 52–53).

For your solo improvisation, keyboards could be used, but if you have string or woodwind players in your class, you may be able to achieve some of the microtones that you hear in Indian music. Alternatively – experiment with improvised singing, and see how many microtonal inflections you are able to sing.

Gamelan music

A gamelan is a set of instruments consisting mainly of tuned gongs, **metallophones** and drums. The instruments of the gamelan are made, tuned and kept together as a set – they are not owned and brought by the individual musicians as happens in most western ensembles. The players do not regard themselves as individual musicians, but as performers on one common instrument.

Gamelan music is heard in many different and diverse contexts, from providing music to accompany shadow puppet plays, poetry, dance and drama to traditional rituals and ceremonies, such as weddings.

Gamelan music in context

A typical Javanese gamelan consists of about 15–20 players, whereas Balinese gamelan ensembles can consist of anything between four and 40 players.

The gamelan comes from the Indonesian islands of Java and Bali in south-east Asia. The instruments that make up a gamelan are not designed to be played solo but always as an ensemble. The word gamelan itself means 'to hammer or handle' and refers to the set of bronze gongs, metallophones (similar to a xylophone), double-headed drums and cymbals.

It is important to note that the Javanese and Balinese gamelan ensembles are different in many ways and have very distinct musical styles. In *GAM*, the music given is that of the Balinese gamelan but during the course of this section we will be looking at aspects of both Javanese and Balinese gamelan music.

Gamelan tradition

In the 19th century the art of gamelan playing in Java was associated mainly with the royal courts of *Surakarta* and *Yogyakarta*. As you might expect, these royal courts possessed the finest gamelans and employed the best players available. Still today some of these gamelans are housed in the courts and are known as ceremonial gamelans.

Many Indonesians consider the music to have magical and mystical properties. The instruments themselves are held in much respect – it is forbidden to step over them, and traditionally offerings of incense are placed before them.

Indonesians believe that each instrument has a soul and a spirit.

Many communities in Java and Bali have their own gamelan ensemble. Traditionally performers are not necessarily professional musicians but are individuals selected to represent their community. Gamelan is an oral tradition – the music is memorised and not learnt from notation. This means that the musicians develop highly advanced aural awareness and memory skills, as learning is achieved through listening, observing and imitating. Each performer within the ensemble is expected to have an understanding of how each instrument works, gaining a knowledge of the whole sound produced by the ensemble. The main concept of the gamelan is that it is one large instrument sounded by many players.

The instruments

Ideally gamelan gongs are made of bronze although often they are made from brass, iron or even bamboo. Traditionally, flowers and leaves are carved on the wooden frames. We will look at a typical Javanese gamelan set-up.

Sometimes, the wooden frames of Javanese gamelans are painted red and gold and there are serpents along the top of the gong poles.

The *balungan* is the core melody. *Balungan* instruments consist of one-octave metallophones including varying sizes of *saron*, metallophones with trough resonators which are played with wooden mallets. The Javanese *balungan* (or Balinese *pokok*) provides the melodic framework for gamelan performances. Above this other instruments (as we shall see below) simultaneously play differently decorated versions of the same melody. This is a texture known as **heterophony** and is one of the characteristic features of gamelan music.

Balungan means 'skeleton'. In Balinese gamelan the equivalent is *pokok* which means 'trunk'.

Beneath the *balungan* are a variety of **gongs**, both hanging and horizontally-mounted. The gongs provide the structure of the cyclic pattern. The largest gong, *gong ageng*, hangs from a frame and ends main cycles. The *kempul* and *kenong*, smaller hanging gongs, divide up main cycles. Horizontally mounted gongs (*kethuk*) signal the smallest units. This continual gong activity marks a passage of time and provides the fundamental metrical framework.

In the third main group are the **embellishing** instruments. Their function is to decorate the *balungan*. *Bonang* are the louder of these so-called 'elaborating' instruments and are rows of horizontally-mounted gong chimes. The group of instruments called *panerusan* are the soft embellishing instruments. These include the *gender* (a metallophone spanning two-and-a-half octaves), a two-string fiddle called a *rebab*, the *suling* (bamboo flute), the *gambang* (wooden xylophone), a plucked zither and singers.

Finally there are the **drums** (*kendhang*). As there is no conductor in this type of music, the drums are the leaders of the ensemble and communicate signals to cue other players, indicate the tempo and dynamics, and emphasise the movements of dancers or puppets.

Java versus Bali

So what are the fundamental differences between Javanese and Balinese gamelan ensembles? If you look at the diagram of a Balinese gamelan in *GAM* (page 120) you will immediately see that many instruments in a Balinese gamelan have different names. You will also notice that some instruments do not appear in one ensemble or the other, and also that some instrument names are the same. The sound worlds of Javanese and Balinese gamelans are quite different. Balinese gamelan music develops more rhythmically – it is more dynamic and has more energy, whereas Javanese gamelan music develops more melodically.

Tuning systems

There are two main tuning systems in gamelan music called *slendro* and *pelog*.

A form of notation is given in *GAM* for clarification. This is a numbering system whereby the approximate pitches are given a number (1, 2, 3, 5, 6 in this case). Dots below the notes indicate the note is to be played in the lower octave, notes above indicate notes in the upper octave. Dots in between the notes indicate rests.

Slendro has five notes which divide the octave into roughly equal segments, each a little larger than a tone. This cannot be accurately expressed in western notation but you can see an approximation on page 119 of *GAM*. The notes show the approximate tuning of the particular gamelan on the recording. Other gamelans will be tuned to quite different pitches for *slendro*.

Pelog is more complicated. There are seven pitches to the octave, but they are in unequal steps ranging from slightly less than a semitone to almost a minor 3rd. In practice only five or six of these notes are used in any one piece. You can see the five *pelog* pitches used in *Jauk Masal* on page 120 of *GAM*. Again, these are the (very approximate) pitches of the gamelan on the recording – other gamelans may be tuned to a quite different set of notes.

Langiang

GAM page 119   CD3 Track 11
Langiang

In *GAM* there are two different pieces of Balinese gamelan music given. The instrumentation in *Langiang* is on a relatively small scale, comprising four two-octave metallophones. One of each pair of metallophones is tuned slightly higher in pitch than the other and this creates acoustic beatings (a wavering, shimmering quality to the sound) when they are played together. The music is based on the pentatonic *slendro* tuning system.

A mellow and gentle sound is created. You should be able to hear the rhythmic cycles at work in this piece. The regularity of the rhythm creates a hypnotic effect.

Jauk Masal

GAM page 120   CD3 Track 12
Jauk Masal

The second piece from *GAM* is called *Jauk Masal* and is quite different from *Langiang* in terms of the instrumentation and the tuning system used in the music. Here we have the *pelog* tuning system. Remember the tunings are only approximate, as some notes can be a quarter (or less) of a tone sharper or flatter than indicated.

The music aims to portray demons and evil spirits. This powerful 'demonic' mood is strongly contrasted to the gentle music of *Langiang*. This is music for dance, and the dancers would wear elaborate masks to depict frightening apparitions. The music creates a restless and tense mood – mainly due to the loud, fast drum signals and the frequent *angsel* (melodic or rhythmic improvisatory sections).

The music is far more sectionalised than the other *GAM* piece and contains a wide exploration of different tempi, including much use of accelerando and rallentando within phrases. Rhythms too are complex and there are some interesting and varied textures created by different combinations of instrumental timbres.

Look at *World Sound Matters*: there is a useful chapter on Indonesian music and recordings of both Javanese and Balinese music.

Test yourself on gamelan music

1. In *Langiang*:

    (i) How would you describe the music at the opening?

    ....

    ....

    (ii) What is played in the lowest part?...................................

    (iii) What is the mood of this piece?....................................

    ....

2. In *Jauk Masal*:

    (i) How would you describe the tempo and dynamics of the music at the start?...

    ....

    (ii) Does the dynamic level vary or remain constant in the music?..

    (iii) What is the of mood of this piece?...................................

    ....

Performing and composing

Using some of the instruments mentioned below, try improvising gamelan music. Arrange the instruments on the floor in the formation of a gamelan and decide on a short nuclear melody (using the notes of a pentatonic scale) that will form the basis of your improvisation. You will obviously not be able to replicate the unique tuning of the gamelan so instead use the pentatonic scale C, D, E, G, A (and no other pitches). See what resources you have available to imitate the sounds of the gamelan. Metallophones, glockenspiels and a vibraphone will be very useful, along with any other metallic percussion you can find. A piano (especially in the upper part of its range), marimba and xylophones will all blend well, and you will need drums and small cymbals. A large gong may be the most difficult instrument to locate, but you may be able to find a synthesised or sampled substitute. Of course, most synthesisers will have a range of metallic tuned percussion sounds that you can draw upon. Remember that a flute and/or violin would also be appropriate in the ensemble. Your teacher will help to direct you in building up

Remember, you should not step over your instruments once you have arranged them – always walk behind them.

layers of sound to create the **heterophonic** texture that characterises gamelan music.

One of the common uses of the gamelan is to accompany shadow puppet plays. Write a short paragraph that tells a simple story (or choose a story or tale that you already know). Now using instruments suggested above, arrange some gamelan music to accompany the puppet play. (Alternatively, you may wish to arrange the gamelan music for electronic keyboards.)

African drumming

As in all parts of the world, there are many different types and styles of music throughout Africa. For this topic we are required to study just the great folk tradition of African drumming in countries such as Ghana. But it is important to remember that the young people of Ghana also have their own types of pop music, including gospel highlife and Afropop, just as the teenagers of Java enjoy American and Indian pop music as well as gamelan.

African drumming in context

Many people associate African music with tribal drumming and indeed the drum is one of the most popular and highly regarded of all African instruments. Drums are often used to accompany singing, dancing and instrumental music.

For your GCSE music course you are required to look at the music of sub-Saharan Africa.

There are many different drums, some played on their own, in pairs or in large ensembles. In the vast area south of the Sahara desert, there exists a multitude of different musical traditions, varying not only from one local district to the next, but also from tribe to tribe. Even the way each drum sounds will vary slightly from one group of performers to the next, meaning that it is very difficult to identify standard practice.

Following their independence, many African countries formed their own drum and dance ensembles as a means of establishing a national identity through music, for example the Djoliba National Ballet of Guinea and the Royal Burundi Drummers.

Role of the drum in African society

One of the most important functions of the drum was for communication. The sound of the drum could travel for miles and traditionally served as a communication link between different tribal communities.

One function of drumming is to bring people together to share common experiences. For every aspect of community life (baptisms, weddings, funerals and so on) there is an accompanying rhythm. This means that if a wedding was taking place, and a certain rhythm was being played, people in a neighbouring village would instantly know what event was happening. Therefore the rhythms all have a social and cultural significance, and members of each community grow up knowing what each rhythm signifies.

Common types of drum

Watch out for names (ie the *dundun*) that can refer to different types of drum in different regions.

African names for drums vary according to region, and even within the same country different names, pronunciation and spellings will be found. Let's take a look at some examples of drums from different countries.

Guinea/Mali	Djembe	A single-headed goblet-shaped drum played with the hands. There will be a solo drum and a set of accompaniment drums, and the tonal range varies depending on the size of each drum.
	Dundun	There are three variants of this double-headed drum played with sticks: **kenkeni**, a high-pitched drum used to keep the pulse; **sangban**, a mid-pitched drum; and **doundoun**, a large double-headed drum.
Senegal	Sabar	A single-headed drum of different sizes and shapes, played with one hand and one stick.
Ghana	Donno	Hourglass 'talking' drum capable of producing a range of pitches. Played under the arm.
	Kagan	Small barrel-shaped drum played with sticks. Is tilted when played.
	Kidi	A medium-sized vertical barrel-shaped drum.

Djembe   Double-headed drum

Playing techniques

A range of pitches and timbres can be produced by playing the drums in different ways, such as:

◆ with sticks

◆ with the hand – to produce slap, tone and bass sounds

◆ by stretching the skin before striking it

◆ leaving the hand or stick on the skin

◆ striking the wood of the drum.

Slap, tone and bass are ways of hitting the drum with the hands. 'Slap' is when the hand strikes the edge of the drum with the fingers spread; 'tone' is when the hand strikes the edge of the drum with the fingers together; and 'bass' is when the main head of the drum is hit with the flat of the hand.

Performance practice

African drumming is based entirely on oral tradition which means that the music has no formal notation. Oral tradition, as a means of learning, leads to local variation in drumming. Two rhythms that have the same name may sound completely different if played by two separate drummers from different communities.

Common features in the music

Some essential features include:

◆ polyrhythms

◆ system of cueing and answering between leader and ensemble

◆ vocalisations (such as shouting)

◆ repetition

◆ varying timbres/techniques possible on the drums.

There is no fixed number of players in a drum ensemble. However a typical drum ensemble will always consist of a lead drummer (or 'master drummer') and an accompaniment section formed by drums of varying pitches and often bells and rattles.

The performance is often started by the leader playing a signal or call which sets the tempo, and tells the ensemble which rhythm to play, and then the accompaniment will begin. This system of musical cueing may happen several times, and serves as a way of

Look at *SM*: piece no 63 features the Royal Burundi Drummers; *World Sound Matters* page 66 features a piece by the Ingoma drum ensemble.

breaking the music up into sections. The performance will be led by the master drummer who maintains the basic rhythm or 'time line'. Against this other drummers play their own rhythmic patterns. The stressed notes in these simultaneous patterns often conflict with each other, producing a polyrhythmic texture.

An important concept to consider when studying African drumming music is tension. The build up of tension is the responsibility of the master drummer who will increase/decrease the tempo and dynamics, and will indicate changes in pitch and rhythm. The tension is the direct result of the complex texture built up from the juxtaposition of simple individual rhythms.

During the course of the music, which in a traditional setting can last from one hour to an all-night performance, each of the individual drummers will take it in turns to play solos while singing and moving to the music. The rest of the group will cheer the centre-stage solo performance and the music continues until each player has had a turn. Drum solos provide a chance for the drummers to show their personality through the drumming, and an opportunity to communicate an emotion. It is the constantly changing performance that maintains interest for the audience and the performers.

You may notice several similarities to the music of mimimalist composers such as Philip Glass and Steve Reich. The latter was fascinated with African drumming and used the technique of repetition with very gradual change in his music.

Structure

Texture
: African drumming is dense and predominantly polyrhythmic.

Cueing
: The leader, or master drummer, will drum a rhythmic pattern to which the other members of the group will respond. This response could include copying, answering or extending the rhythm instigated by the lead drummer. This is a type of cue for the whole group. If you look at *Nzekele*, you can see how a rhythmic cue is used (for example at letter B) to provoke a response from the ensemble. Can you find another cue in this piece? Is it played by the same drummer?

Repetition with variation
: The music might initially sound very repetitive but listen carefully and you will hear constant variations of basic patterns. Development is an important part of African drumming – as the music is repeated, individual players may develop certain rhythmic ideas.

Cross-rhythms
: An important feature of African drumming is the use of cross-rhythms, in which two or more different rhythms conflict with one another. In a performance, a larger number of rhythms will be layered creating even more tension. Another example can be seen in the middle two bars of the bottom stave of page 129 of *GAM*.

Syncopation
: Syncopation occurs when an accent is placed on a beat that is normally unaccented.

Rhythmic cycles
: Rhythmic cycles are repeated rhythm patterns. They are often based on speech patterns. Some beats are more strongly emphasised than others, and certain beats are played with differing parts

of the hand or stick to create different timbres. The length of each rhythmic cycle is not fixed, but will usually be of a short duration. It is the combination of different rhythmic cycles in different metres that produces the polyrhythmic texture of the music.

Kundum

In *Kundum* there are two dances, one slow and the other fast. The master drum opens each dance with solo improvisations. A metal bell, called the *dawuro*, and a rattle, called *ntroa* keeps the basic accompanying rhythm going in both dances. You can see details of these rhythms in the *GAM*. The varying rhythmic patterns produce a polyrhythmic texture and in the opening slow section you can hear combinations of rhythmic patterns in both duple and triple times played simultaneously, thereby creating cross rhythms. To the accompaniment of this polyrhythmic texture, the master drummer improvises his solos. Much the same applies to the fast section where the master drummer plays one- and two-bar syncopated rhythms against the other parts.

| *GAM page 124* | CD3 Track 15 |
| *Kundum* | |

Nzekele

In *Nzekele* you can follow a transcribed score. African drumming is notoriously difficult to notate as some of the rhythms are not exact in metrical terms. However the *GAM* extract gives a good idea of the complex textures created in this piece and it allows you to see how cross-rhythms arise. This is an exciting piece to listen to and the opening virtuoso solo display by the master drummer sets the tone for the rest of the piece. In this section we can hear the complex syncopated patterns that arise from the drummer accenting the first, fourth and seventh semiquaver in each bar. Several times during the piece, you will hear a rhythmic cue given by a lead drummer and then a unison riff played by the other drum parts. This can be likened to African singing where the leader 'calls' the line and is given a tribal 'response'. Call and response is a common technique used in all forms of African music. In the fast section (letter E in the score) the regularity of the basic accompanying rhythm and the driving quaver-rhythms are replaced by a more diverse section with solos performed by different drummers.

| *GAM page 126* | CD3 Track 16 |
| *Nzekele* | |

Test yourself on African drumming

1. (i)   What do you understand by rhythmic cueing?

    ....

    ....

    (ii) What are polyrhythms?...

    ....

2. What is the role of the master drummer?...............................

    ....

    ....

    ....

3. (i) Name two types of African drum.

....

....

(ii) Describe two ways in which the drum can be played.

....

....

4. (i) Describe two features found in **both** *Kundum* and *Nzekele* that are typical of African drumming. ....

....

....

....

(ii) Which piece did you prefer? Give a musical reason for your choice. ....

....

....

....

Performing

Have a go at performing a polyrhythmic piece. Form a group of four or more players, give each player a different percussion instrument and divide into two groups. Group 1 must decide upon a simple rhythm in a four-beat cycle ($\frac{4}{4}$ time), group 2 must decide upon a simple rhythm in a three-beat cycle ($\frac{3}{4}$ time). Both groups try playing their rhythms at the same time keeping to the same crotchet pulse. See *left* for two rhythms you could try. The effect should be that of conflicting rhythms. At an agreed number of repetitions, each player could try a new pattern to add variety. Record your piece and listen to the group's efforts. Was there a point where the rhythms came into phase with one another?

Composing

If you are pleased with the piece you have created try notating it as a score. Compare the polyrhythmic texture you have created with that of *Nzekele* (*GAM* page 126).

Music which draws together at least two different cultures

This topic is diverse and wide ranging as there are many types of music that have drawn together at least two different cultures. In simple terms, this is often referred to as fusion. These fusions have created new styles of music that have become established in their own rights.

Bhangra

Bhangra is now known as a type of modern British-Asian popular dance music that combines the traditional melodies and rhythms of Indian bhangra, with the western instruments and techniques used in club dance culture. However the origins of bhangra go back a long way.

Bhangra started life as the music of field workers in the Punjab region of India. This music was performed during the festival of *bisakh* to celebrate the end of the harvest. Originally the music was accompanied by the *dhol*, a double-ended wooden barrel-drum. The instrument was capable of playing quite complicated cross-rhythms between the hands, which gave the music its characteristic swinging rhythms and provided the essential dance groove of the music. The characteristic rhythm of bhangra is an eight-beat rhythmic cycle called the *chaal* and is still used in modern bhangra today, *right*.

The music became more popular and gradually moved from the rural farming communities to the towns, where it was used for entertainment. The transformation of bhangra from a popular, local style into a mass-produced music with western influences, took place in this country in the late 1970s. Post-war immigrants to Britain brought the rhythms and melodies of bhangra with them. Young Asians in Britain at the time were keen to forge an identity for themselves and bhangra provided that identity. The rhythmic element originally played on the *dhol* made its transition to the drum machine with virtually no changes.

Modern bhangra has developed primarily as a dance music and music technology now plays an important role in its creation.

Mundian To Bach Ke

Mundian To Bach Ke characteristically mixes Asian and western elements with the use of traditional as well as electronic instruments. Some common electronic techniques are used, for example the use of looped material throughout the song. The structure is a verse-chorus pattern, with the additional sections of introduction, bridge and a short coda section. The vocal part is also fairly typical of the style. The range is very limited. The largest interval is a minor 3rd (E♭ to G♭) and the melodic line, as such, is not only limited in pitch but equally is extremely repetitive.

Salsa

The Caribbean islands of Cuba and Puerto Rico were settled by the Spanish who (like the British in Jamaica) imported many Africans to work as slaves. As a result the traditional music of these islands is a unique blend of Spanish and African traditions, giving the world many new dance styles such as the conga, rumba, mambo and cha-cha-cha. These dances are often described as 'Latin-American' – a term that refers to those areas of America (South America, Central America and some Caribbean islands) where Spanish or Portugese is the predominant language and culture.

Salsa is a lively dance style that combines Latin-American rhythms with the instrumentation of American big-band jazz. It thus brings together features of music from Spain, Africa, the Caribbean and the USA.

Origins

The predominant crop was hemp, or in Indian *bhang*, so you can see where the name came from.

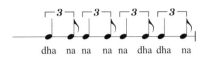

dha na na na na dha dha na

na = play the treble side of the dhol.
dha = play the bass and treble sides together

GAM page 136	CD3 Track 18
Mundian To Bach Ke	

Bernstein included a mambo and a cha-cha-cha in the 'The Dance at the Gym' in *West Side Story*.

Origins of salsa

Claves

The root of salsa is the *son*, a type of traditional vocal music in Cuba and Puerto Rico. The influences of traditional Spanish music include a verse-and-chorus format, simple harmonies often based on tonic-and-dominant chord patterns in a minor key, and the use of instruments such as the acoustic guitar and double bass. The African influences are apparent in the use of syncopated rhythms, call-and-response dialogue between a soloist (*prégon*) and a chorus (*coro*), and percussion instruments (claves, bongos and maracas) that are of African origin. An example of *son* is the piece *Se quema la chumbamba*, which is to be found in *NAM* and *The Rough Guide to Salsa* CD mentioned later.

Son clave

The most important rhythmic element in *son* is the clave pattern. The claves are a pair of wooden sticks and normally play the rhythm (known as *son* clave) shown *left*.

This pattern consists of three notes in the first bar and two in the second, and is therefore known as *3:2 son clave*. If the two bars are reversed, so that the pattern starts with the bar of two notes, it is called *2:3 son clave*.

Page 126 of GAM

The African origin of *son clave* is clear if we notate it in half-note values, as shown on the second stave, *left*. We can then see that it is precisely the same as the clave rhythm of African drumming shown on page 126 of *GAM*.

Rumba clave

Son was originally performed by groups of six or seven musicians, but during the 1950s the bands became larger and their repertoire extended to dances such as the mambo and rumba. The latter has a characteristic rhythm called *rumba clave* (shown *left*), which is a variant of the original *son* pattern. Around these basic clave patterns, other Latin-American percussion instruments (such as bongos and maracas) and the vocalist weave their own syncopated rhythms, often creating a texture of elaborate cross-rhythms.

Jazz influences on salsa

Following a communist revolution in 1959 Cuba became isolated from most of the western world. The development of contemporary Latin-American dance music was then continued by Puerto Ricans living in New York. It was here that features of big-band jazz were incorporated into the son-rumba mix, and it was here that the name salsa was first used to describe this new fusion. Salsa means 'sauce' and it perhaps refers to the spicy elements of jazz that enlivened the Latin-American style.

Salsa was not the first fusion between jazz and Cuban music. In the late 1940s Dizzy Gillespie was famous for his Afro-Cuban style of jazz. Jazz is music for listening, while salsa is music for dancing, but both these types of fusion reunite Cuban music and jazz with their common roots in the rhythms of Africa.

The most obvious influence of big-band jazz is in the use of a much larger ensemble for salsa. Typically there would be 15 performers, divided into a frontline (three trumpets and two trombones) and a large rhythm section (drum kit, congas, timbales, bongos, maracas, piano, bass and often baritone saxophone), plus usually two singers. Also from jazz came the use of much more complex harmonies and scat singing by the vocalists – this is a jazz-singing technique that involves improvising to nonsense syllables.

A good introduction to salsa can be found on the CD *The Rough Guide to Salsa* from the World Music Network (RGNET1017CD).

Clave patterns, syncopation, cross-rhythms, riffs, Latin-American percussion and brilliant brass arrangements all continue to play an important part in salsa, which is usually played at a lively tempo since it is primarily music for energetic dancing.

Lou Harrison

Lou Harrison (1917–2003) grew up on the Pacific coast, where he came under the influence of both western and non-western music. He worked with two key 20th-century composers, Arnold Schoenberg and John Cage. Harrison travelled widely, continually adding to his ability to draw on other cultural traditions in his work. Indeed he once said: 'It is no longer apropos to know just the music that you were raised in, but you must know one other. Otherwise you are not a citizen of the 20th-century world.' Harrison experimented even as a boy with new ways of organising pitch and rhythm. He said that he would like to stop composing for the western system of tones and semitones, and for western instruments. He also became impatient with what he sees as the metrically unimaginative nature of western music.

Harrison has long been interested in dance, theatre and puppets: no wonder he was drawn by gamelan.

Suite for Violin, Piano and Small Orchestra: Second Gamelan

Harrison's early compositions included music for percussion which combines western and non-western influences. Recordings introduced him to Indonesian gamelan music and he set out to construct 'American gamelans' using instruments built to emulate Balinese timbres and tunings. Nevertheless this suite (written at 34), though inspired by Balinese gamelan music, is written for traditional western instruments. All the same, you can definitely find gamelan characteristics here. It starts with a minimalist ostinato figure, then two bars later the next layer of sound is pentatonic movement, with lots of movement in parallel 4ths, creating a far-eastern sound.

Do you notice the way that the ostinato celeste and tack-piano bass line changes in bar 20? Notice the D.C. marked in bar 50 which sends you back to bar 3: would the resulting ABA structure justify your saying the piece is in ternary form? Now contrast these A and B sections: can you find adjectives to describe their sound colours and mood? You might think that A is punchier and B is more legato. But why? Look at the articulation and dynamic contrast for the answer.

GAM page 13   CD3 Track 17
Suite for Violin, Piano and Small
Orchestra: Second Gamelan
Lou Harrison (1917–2003)

Don't panic if you think you've lost the violin of the title: it just doesn't turn up in this movement!

Lou Harrison's Suite is included on *Looking to the East*, CRI CD 836, which also includes works by three other American composers with their eyes on non-western musical styles and traditions, Cowell, McPhee and Hovhaness. McPhee was a pioneer in introducing gamelan to western ears. If Harrison's music catches your interest, look for *Pacifica Rondo* and *La Koro Sutro* for chorus and gamelan.

Test yourself on music that draws together at least two different cultures

1. (i) Bhangra is a synthesis of musical elements from which two different cultures?..

....

....

    (ii) What name is given to the characteristic rhythm used in bhangra?..

2. In *Mundian To Bach Ke*:

    (i) What instruments play in the introduction?

....

    (ii) Name an electronic instrument that is used.

....

(iii) What mood do you think is conveyed in the music?

....

....

....

(iv) Which features of this piece are Indian in origin and which come from western music? ....

....

....

....

3. (i) Salsa is a fusion of which musical cultures?

....

(ii) Write out a son-clave pattern. ....

....

....

(iii) List three musical elements present in salsa. ....

....

....

4. In *Se quema la chumbamba*:

(i) Which of the following best describes the music's tonality?
Minor   Pentatonic   Major   Atonal

(ii) Name three instruments playing in the extract.

....

....

....

(iii) What is the name of the traditional clave rhythm that is featured in this piece? ....

5. (i) Find three musical characteristics that show the 'elegant simplicity' of Harrison's Suite for Violin, Piano and Small Orchestra. ....

....

....

....

(ii) What musical characteristics can you point to that show Harrison composing in gamelan style in his Suite?

....

....

(iii) Ring any of the following terms which best describe Harrison's Suite:

modal   repetitive   atonal   minimalist
syncopated   aleatoric   complex   consonant

Performing

Set up a group of players in a semicircle with an assortment of percussion instruments (as described in the composing section below).

One person acting as leader should sit in the centre of the group and start the improvisation by playing a son-clave rhythm. The leader will then indicate (through nodding) to someone else in the group to come in with their own ostinato rhythm against the established clave pattern. One by one, the players enter and eventually you will have built up several layers of rhythms.

The vocalist should then improvise a melodic part using vocalise, ie no words but using various vowel sounds, such as 'Ah'.

Composing

Using a combination of traditional and electronic instruments, compose a short dance piece in bhangra style. Use the characteristic *chaal* rhythm and the structure of *Mundian To Bach Ke* – compose a short introduction, then a verse followed by a chorus, and finish off with a short coda section. You may of course write more than one verse: that's up to you. Sequencers, keyboards, and samplers can be used to produce appropriate backings in bhangra style. If you are pleased with your efforts, try to arrange a performance of the completed composition to your class. Ask them to comment on its effectiveness as a fusion of styles. You might want to revise your work in light of some of their ideas.

Sample questions

In the listening exam you will have to answer questions on 12 extracts of music played on CD. These extracts will be related to the topics you have covered in the four Areas of Study but they are unlikely to come from the specific pieces you have studied.

The following sample questions are intended to give you an idea of what to expect. Most music departments will have recordings of the works concerned. Some questions need only one-word answers, but where a longer response is required it is important that you show that you can use musical vocabulary accurately. Also try to support your opinions by referring to specific features and events that you hear in the music. To illustrate these points we have shown a possible answer to question 1(d) below – it is not the only correct answer of course.

TIP: Every year candidates hope to cover their uncertainty by ticking or underlining more than one answer in multiple-choice questions. This will result in no marks at all. If you really are undecided you would do better to take a guess. When checking your answers make sure that any incorrect rough markings on the paper are properly erased so that the examiner is in no doubt about what you mean.

In the exam there will be a short pause between each repetition of the extract and after the final playing you will be given two minutes to complete your answers. You can start writing as soon as the music begins. A good strategy is lightly to pencil in the shorter answers as you listen (being careful to check their accuracy on subsequent repetitions). Make brief rough notes for the longer questions and use the two minutes at the end to ink in your final conclusions. Make sure that your answers are not ambiguous (see *left*) – if they are you will probably not get a mark. Finally, read the questions carefully. For instance, if you include your answer to (c) below in your answer to (d) it will not get a mark because you are asked to find other differences.

AREA OF STUDY 1   Repetition and contrast in Western Classical Music 1600–1899

1. Listen **THREE TIMES** to the theme and first variation from the last movement of Mozart's Quintet in A major, K581.

    (a) The theme is introduced by two violins. Name the woodwind instrument that then joins in.

    ....

    (b) Underline the term that best describes the theme:

    Atonal   Major key   Minor key   Modal   Mainly chromatic

    (c) At the start of Variation 1 the theme is repeated, but what is added?

    ....

    (d) Describe **THREE** other ways in which Variation 1 differs from the theme.

    The second phrase of the theme is now an octave lower on viola and cello. ....

    The melody of the theme is missing at the start of the second section, although the harmony is the same. ...

    The variation is more chromatic than the theme, especially at the end. ....

2. Listen **TWICE** to the air 'If With All Your Hearts', No. 4 from Mendelssohn's *Elijah*.
   Here are the words (which are repeated several times) of the first two sections:

   A   If with all your hearts ye truly seek me, ye shall ever surely find me, thus saith our God.

   B   Oh! that I knew where I might find him that I might even come before his presence.

   (a) Underline **two** terms that describe what you hear in the accompaniment of the first phrase:

   scales   arpeggios   pedal   ground bass   syncopation   imitation

   (b) What is the main way in which the B section contrasts with the A section?

   ....

   ....

   (c) Name the form of the entire air. ....

   (d) Underline the type of voice heard in this piece:

   treble   soprano   alto   tenor   bass   falsetto

AREA OF STUDY 2   New Directions in Western Classical Music – 1900 to the present day

3. Listen **THREE TIMES** to the first four phrases of *Song for Athene* by John Tavener.

   > There is bargain-price recording of this piece on Naxos 8.555256.

   Here is phrase 1, followed by the words of phrases 2–4.

Phrase 1 — Al - le - lu - - i - a,_____ al - le - lu - i - a.

Phrase 2   May flights of angels sing thee to thy rest.

Phrase 3   Alleluia, alleluia.

Phrase 4   Remember me O lord, when you come into your kingdom.

   (a) In what key is phrase 1? ....

   (b) How does phrase 2 relate to phrase 1? ....

   (c) How does phrase 3 differ from phrase 1? ....

   (d) The texture of phrase 4 is the same as the texture of which other phrase? ....

   (e) Underline **three** terms below that correctly describe this music:

   aria   a cappella   polyphonic   unmetrical   serial   homophonic   atonal   pentatonic

   (f) Briefly describe how Tavener creates a mood of stillness and serenity in this extract.

   ....

   ....

   ....

   ....

   ....

(g) Tavener is sometimes called a 'holy minimalist'. Describe any features of the piece that justify this label. ....

....

....

....

....

....

....

AREA OF STUDY 3   Popular Song in Context

4. Listen **THREE TIMES** to the first 54 seconds of *Can't Buy Me Love* by the Beatles. The extract consists of the following four sections:

Intro	Verse 1	Verse 2	Refrain

(a) The hook line 'Can't buy me love' is heard twice at the start. Which of the following best describes the setting of these words? Tick the box next to your chosen answer.

☐ A scalic melody accompanied by major chords

☐ A scalic melody accompanied by minor chords

☐ A melody based on a major triad, accompanied by major chords

☐ A melody based on a major triad, accompanied by minor chords

(b) Where else in the extract is this hook line heard? ....

(c) Name two ways in which this song has been influenced by the 12-bar blues.

....

....

....

....

(d) Write a short paragraph describing the origins of the 12-bar blues.

....

....

....

....

....

....

AREA OF STUDY 4   Rhythms, scales and modes in music from around the world

5. Listen **TWICE** to *Madhuvani* rāg played
    by Ali Akbar Khan on sarod.

> An extract of this recording is available on Navras' Sampler CD No. 7 from Navras Records (www.navrasrecords.com). Navras produce eight sampler CDs which contain many samples of Indian classical, folk and popular music.

   (a) Is the sarod bowed or plucked? ....

   (b) What other instrument can you hear? ....

   (c) Briefly describe the form of this extract. ....
   ....
   ....
   ....
   ....

   (d) *Madhuvani* is supposed to be performed in the afternoon. Describe how the atmosphere of a hot,
        sultry afternoon is created, referring specifically to mood, melody and rhythm.
   ....
   ....
   ....
   ....
   ....

Glossary

Remember that you are expected to use technical terms correctly and you should be able to identify something when you hear it.

A cappella. Unaccompanied singing (usually choral).

Additive rhythm. Rhythmic patterns made from repetitions of a fast note-value as opposed to rhythms based on divisions and multiplications of the time value of a regular pulse. Fast quavers grouped 3+3+2 or 3+2+3 (perhaps with an $\frac{8}{8}$ time signature) are additive rhythms as opposed to metrical rhythms, such as a minim plus four quavers in $\frac{4}{4}$ time.

Agogo bells. Struck clapperless bells found in African and Latin-American music.

Air. English or French for a song.

Alap. In Indian music, an unmetred improvised prelude.

Aleatoric. Determined by chance rather than by the decision of the composer.

Alto. A high male or low female voice.

Antiphony. Music in which two or more groups of performers alternate with each other.

Arpeggio. A chord played as successive rather than simultaneous notes.

Articulation. 1. The point at which a note is sounded. **2.** The length of notes in relation to their context (eg legato as opposed to staccato articulation).

Atonal music. Music that is unrelated to a tonic note and so has no sense of key.

Authentic performance. A performance that takes account of historical performance practice using instruments of the time or replicas based on contemporary descriptions.

Bar. A metrical unit represented in print by all of the notes and rests between vertical lines called barlines.

Baroque. The period c.1600–1750 and its music.

Basic series, Basic set. The original 12-note row of a serial composition. Also known as the prime or prime order.

Bass. 1. A low male voice. **2.** The lowest-sounding part of a composition whether for voices or instruments.

Basso continuo. In baroque music, a continuous bass part, often with figures to indicate the chords that should be improvised on a harmony instrument such as a harpsichord or organ. The basso continuo is often played on a melody bass instrument such as a cello or bassoon. Not to be confused with basso ostinato.

Basso ostinato. A short bass melody continuously repeated throughout an entire movement or lengthy passage of a movement. Not to be confused with basso continuo.

Baya. The larger of the pair of Indian drums called a **tabla**.

Beam. A line joining the stems of two or more notes, such as quavers.

Beat. The underlying pulse of metrical music.

Bhangra. An amalgamation of western pop styles and traditional Punjabi styles of music.

Binary form. A musical structure in two sections (AB).

Blue note. See **Blues scale.**

Blues scale. A scale in which some pitches (blue notes) are performed slightly flatter than their counterparts in a major scale. The most commonly altered pitches are the third and seventh degrees.

Bpm. Abbreviation of beats per minute.

Break. In pop music and jazz, a solo linking-phrase that is usually improvised. In club music, a passage in which the beat is suspended and replaced by sound effects or solos.

Cadence. A point of repose at the end of a phrase, sometimes harmonised with two cadence chords. See **perfect cadence**, **imperfect cadence**, **plagal cadence** and **interrupted cadence**.

Cadenza. An improvised or written-out solo in an aria or concerto movement.

Call and response. A technique whereby a soloist sings or plays a phrase to which a larger group responds with an answering phrase.

Canon. A compositional device in which a melody in one part is later repeated note for note in another part while the melody in the first part continues to unfold.

Canon by inversion. A canon in which the second part to enter presents the original melody upside down.

Cantabile. In a singing style.

Cantata. A baroque sacred or secular vocal composition in several sections or movements.

Celempung. Large zither played in a Javanese gamelan.

Cell. Another term for a **motif**. It most often refers to a small group of notes or a short rhythm in some 20th-century modernist styles.

Chaal rhythm. Basic rhythm found in **bhangra**.

Chaconne and passacaglia. Though different in their origins, by the beginning of the 18th century there was little difference between these two forms. Both were continuous variations based on an ostinato which could be a repeating bass pattern, a harmonic progression or both.

Chamber music. Music intended for domestic performance with one instrument per part.

Choir. A group of singers performing together, whether in unison or in parts.

Chorale. A Protestant hymn tune with German words.

Chorale prelude. An organ composition based on the melody of a **chorale**.

Chorus. 1. In popular music, a setting of the **refrain** of the lyrics. **2.** A large group of singers usually performing compositions in several parts. **3.** The electronic multiplication of an individual part to give it greater body.

Chromatic notes. See **Diatonic and chromatic notes**.

Clave rhythm. In salsa, the central rhythmic pattern underlying the entire structure of the music, around which the other parts must fit. The rhythm is usually played on a pair of wooden sticks called claves.

Clef. A symbol defining the pitches of the notes on a stave.

Coda. The final section of a movement or piece.

Collage. A composition in which different sound events are added together or overlapped with each other.

Concerto. A composition for one or more solo instruments accompanied by an orchestra. Usually in three movements.

Concord. See **Consonance and dissonance**.

Consonance and dissonance. The relative stability (consonance) or instability (dissonance) of two or more notes sounded simultaneously. Consonant intervals and chords are called concords. Dissonant intervals and chords are called discords.

Contrary motion. The relationship between two melodies in which an ascent in one part is mirrored by a simultaneous descent in the other part, and vice versa.

Countermelody. A new melody that occurs simultaneously with a melody that has been heard before.

Counterpoint. The simultaneous combination of two or more melodic lines.

Countersubject. A melody sounding against and contrasting with the subject or answer of a fugue or similar contrapuntal composition.

Cross rhythm. A rhythm that conflicts with the regular pattern of stressed and unstressed beats of a composition, or the combination of two conflicting rhythms within a single beat (eg duplets against triplets).

Decks. Turntables used by DJs.

Decoration. Printed embellishments or small departures from the written score intended to enrich a performance and provide variety in repeated passages.

Descant. A decorative line sung above the main melody of a hymn or similar vocal piece.

Dhol. A large cylindrical south Asian drum.

Diatonic and chromatic notes. Diatonic notes are those belonging to the scale of the prevailing key while chromatic notes are foreign to it. For example, in C major G is a diatonic note whereas G♯ is a chromatic note.

Discord. See **Consonance and dissonance**.

Dissonance. See **Consonance and dissonance**.

Divisions. A type of variation form in which the long notes of the theme are divided into shorter note values by the addition of extra notes.

Djembe. Goblet-shaped west-African drum.

Dodecaphony, Serial music, Twelve-tone music. Music derived from a pre-determined set of 12 different **pitch classes**.

Dominant. The fifth degree of a major or minor scale (eg D is the dominant in G major).

Dominant pedal. The fifth degree of a scale held or repeated against changing harmony.

Dominant 7th chord. A chord consisting of the dominant – the fifth degree of the scale – plus diatonic notes a 3rd, 5th and 7th above it. In C major the dominant 7th chord consists of the notes G, B, D and F.

Double stopping. The performance of a two-note chord on a bowed string instrument.

Doubling. The simultaneous performance of the same melody by two players or groups of players, either at the same pitch or at pitch levels separated by octaves.

Drone. The same as **pedal**, but the term is usually associated with folk music. A two-note drone often consists of the tonic and dominant.

Drum and bass. Very fast popular dance style – drum and bass indicates the underlying structure.

Drum machine. A synthesiser capable of simulating the sounds of a number of percussion instruments.

Dubbing. Copying of recorded sound and adding it to, or mixing it with, a different sound source.

Dynamics. The loudness (f) and quietness (p) of notes.

Enharmonics. Two notes of the same pitch that are notated differently, eg C and B♯.

Episode. A distinct section within a movement.

Falsetto. A special vocal technique that enables a man to extend his range to higher pitches than usual.

Figuration. A melodic line made up of repeated figures or continuous ornamental patterns.

Figure. Another name for a **motif**.

Figured bass. A bass part with Arabic numerals that indicate the intervals above the bass that are to be played in order to form the desired chords.

Flat. 1. A sign (♭) which lowers the pitch of a note a semitone. One or more flat signs at the beginning of a stave make a key signature. Each flat in a key signature lowers notes with the same letter name by a semitone throughout the rest of the stave. A flat inserted immediately in front of a note is an accidental, and its effect only lasts until the end of the bar. **2.** An adjective describing a note that is sung or played at a lower pitch than it should be.

Frets. Raised strips running at right angles across the fingerboard of instruments such as the guitar, lute and sitar.

Fugue. A composition based on a melody (called the subject) that is repeated in combination with a rhythmically independent countersubejct.

Fusion. Music in which two or more styles are blended together, for example bhangra.

Gamba. See **viola da gamba**.

Gat. In north Indian music, an instrumental composition.

Genre. A category or group such as the piano sonata.

Glissando. A slide from one pitch to another.

Gong. A large circular metal plate suspended in a frame and beaten with a stick or a mallet.

Gong-chimes. Sets of knobbed gong-kettles in a gamelan.

Gospel. An emotional style of African-American song deriving from Protestant hymns based on texts from the four biblical Gospels. The style includes spontaneous often syncopated ornamentation, with blue notes, stamping and clapping, and congregational interjections such as 'Yes Lord'.

Grace notes. Any of the many melodic ornaments printed in small type near to a principal melody note.

Graphic score. A written account of a piece of music that uses pictorial means rather than conventional notation to indicate matters like pitch and duration.

Groove. Repetitive, cyclic rhythm patterns (eg on a drum machine).

Ground bass. A melody in the bass part of a composition that is repeated many times and which forms the basis for a continuous set of melodic and/or harmonic variations.

Harmonic progression. A series of chords.

Harmonium. A reed organ, once found in churches and now used in some Indian music.

Harpsichord. A keyboard instrument with one, two or three manuals controlling a set of jacks. Each jack has a quill or piece of plastic that plucks a string when a key is depressed.

Heterophony. A texture made up of a simple tune and a more elaborate version of it played or sung together.

Homophony. A texture in which one (usually the uppermost) part has all of the melodic interest, while the others provide a simple accompaniment.

Hook. In pop music, a short melodic idea that is designed to be instantly memorable.

Imitation. A contrapuntal device in which a melodic idea stated in one part is copied in another part while the melodic line of the first part continues. Only the opening notes of the original melody need to be repeated for this effect to be heard.

Imperfect cadence. An approach chord plus chord V at the end of a phrase.

Improvisation. Performance based not on a written score but on the mood of the moment.

Interrupted cadence. Chord V followed by an unexpected chord (such as VI) at the end of a phrase.

Interval. The distance between two pitches, including both of the pitches that form the interval. So, in the scale of C major, the interval between the first and second notes is a 2nd (C–D), the interval between the first and third notes is a 3rd (C–D–E), and so on.

Inversion. 1. The process of turning a melody upside down so that every interval of the original is maintained but moves in the opposite direction. **2.** A chord is inverted when a note other than the root is sounded in the bass. **3.** An interval is inverted when one of the two notes moves an octave so that instead of being below the second note it is above it (or vice versa).

Jazz quavers. See **Swing quavers, swung quavers**.

Jhala. In north Indian music, a lively, rhythmical improvised section in fast tempo following the **jhor** section.

Jhor. In north Indian music, an improvisatory section in medium tempo following the **alap** that has a strong pulse but no set metre.

Key. The relationship between the pitches of notes in which one particular pitch called the **tonic** seems more important than any other pitch. The pitch of the tonic determines the key of the music. So a composition in which C is the tonic is 'in the key of C'.

Key signature. One or more flat signs, or one or more sharp signs placed immediately after a clef at the beginning of a stave. The effect of each sign lasts throughout the stave and applies to all notes of the same pitch class. In many cases a key signature gives some indication of the key of the music printed on the same stave.

Leap. An interval greater than a semitone or tone between consecutive notes of a melody.

Legato. A smooth articulation of music without any breaks between successive notes.

Loop. See **Tape loop.**

Lute. A fretted plucked-string instrument popular in the renaissance and baroque periods, used for solo performance and accompaniment.

Lyrics. The text of a song including songs from musicals.

Major and minor. Greater and lesser. A major interval is greater than a minor interval by a semitone. The interval between the first and third degrees of a major scale is four semitones, one semitone greater than the interval between the same degrees in a minor scale.

Master drum. The drum played by the leader of an African percussion group (the master drummer).

Melodic inversion. See **Inversion 1.**

Melody and accompaniment. The melody is the line of a piece of music where choice and arrangement of pitch, duration and intervals are intended to provide primary interest. It is often played on higher instruments, for example violin, flute, trumpet (and piano right hand). The accompaniment is the part or parts of the music which supports the melody. It is initially less noticeable, partly because it tends to be written on deeper-sounding instruments, eg trombone, double bass (and piano left hand).

Mento. A Jamaican song or dance. It has a lively, syncopated rhythm often with the accent placed on the fourth beat of the bar.

Metallophone. A category of musical instruments consisting of rows of tuned metal bars that are struck with mallets.

Metre. The repeating patterns produced by strong and weak pulses, usually of the same duration.

Microtone. An interval smaller than a semitone.

Middle eight. A contrasting section in the middle of a song (not necessarily eight bars long).

MIDI. Musical Instrument Digital Interface: a system for exchanging music performance data between suitably equipped computers and/or electronic instruments.

Minimalism. A style of the late 20th century. It was a reaction against the complexities of modernist compositional styles and was characterised by the varied repetition of simple rhythmic, melodic or harmonic ideas.

Minuet. An elegant dance in $\frac{3}{4}$, it was the only dance of the baroque suite to be retained in classical instrumental music where it formed a ternary movement with a trio.

Modal music. Music based on one of the scales of seven pitch classes commonly found in western music, but excluding the major and minor scales.

Modulation. The harmonic or melodic process by which music moves from one key to another.

Monophony. A single unaccompanied melody which may be performed by a soloist or by many people playing or singing the melody in unison or in octaves.

Motif. A short melodic or rhythmic idea that is sufficiently distinctive to allow it to be modified, manipulated and possibly combined with other motifs while retaining its own identity.

Multi-tracking. A recording technique where several tracks of sound are recorded independently but can be played back together.

Note row. See **Tone row.**

Octave. The interval between the first and last degrees of an eight-note major or minor scale. The two notes forming this interval are 12 semitones apart and have the same letter name.

Octave displacement. The practice of moving notes of a tone row one or more octaves from their original pitches, thus producing the angular melodic lines that are typical of most serial compositions.

Octave equivalence. The idea that any note of a pitch class functions in the same way as the original pitch in a tone row no matter which octave it appears in.

Ode. In baroque music, a setting of a lyric poem addressed to St Cecilia or to some important person such as the reigning monarch. Like the cantata it contains several vocal movements.

On-beat and off-beat notes. Notes articulated on strong and weak beats of the bar respectively.

Opera. A dramatic fusion of words, music, spectacle and sometimes dancing.

Oral tradition. Music handed down from one generation to another by speech and performance rather than by notation and writing.

Oratorio. A vocal setting of a sacred text falling into many movements and intended for concert rather than dramatic performance.

Ostinato. A rhythmic, melodic or harmonic pattern repeated many times in succession. Often called a **riff** in pop music.

Overdotting. In baroque music, the performance practice of adding a second dot to a dotted note value and, consequently, shortening the value of the note that follows it.

Passacaglia. See **Chaconne and passacaglia.**

Passing note. A decorative melody note filling the gap between two harmony notes.

Pedal. A sustained or repeated note sounded against changing harmony.

Pelog. A tuning system, usually of seven pitches, used in Indonesian gamelan music.

Pentatonic music. Music based on a scale of five notes.

Perfect cadence. Chords V and I at the end of a phrase.

Phrase. Part of a melody which requires the addition of another phrase or phrases to make complete musical sense.

Piano. 1. A keyboard instrument in which strings are sounded by felt-covered hammers. **2.** A dynamic instruction to play softly.

Pitch. The height or depth of a note. This can be relative and expressed as an interval (such as a tone or semitone) between two notes, or it can be an absolute quality determined by the number of vibrations per second of a string, a column of air or a membrane.

Pitch bending. Detuning a note so it slides to another pitch.

Pitch class. A set of pitches all having the same letter name. So middle C belongs to the same pitch class as the C an octave below and the C an octave above it.

Pitch names. The letters from A to G which are used to identify the pitches of notes on a stave. See **pitch class**.

Plagal cadence. Chords IV and I at the end of a phrase.

Pointillism. A 20th-century style in which a succession of isolated notes are heard as points of sound similar to the dots of colour in pointillist paintings.

Pokok. The melodic essence of a piece played on a gamelan orchestra.

Polyphony. As used most frequently today polyphony means the same as counterpoint – a texture made up of two or more melodies sounding together.

Polyrhythm. The simultaneous combination of two or more distinctly different and often conflicting types of rhythm.

Primary triads. Chords I, IV and V.

Prime, Prime order. See **Basic series**.

Programme music. Music that is meant to suggest visual images or a story.

Pulse. Beat.

Quintuplet. A group of five equal notes played in the time usually taken by four notes of the same time values.

Rāg (raga). A pattern of ascending and descending notes associated with particular moods and used as the basis for melodic improvisation in Indian classical music.

Range. The distance between the lowest and highest notes of a melody or composition, or the distance between the highest and lowest notes that can be played on an instrument or vocalist.

Recapitulation. The repetition of music heard earlier in the same movement, notably a movement in sonata form.

Refrain. A repeated passage of music.

Register. A part of the range of a voice or instrument. The lowest pitches of a clarinet are in the chalumeau register. The highest pitches of a baroque trumpet are in the clarino register.

Repetition. In music, the re-statement of a passage that has already been performed.

Retrograde. A series of note values, pitches or chords played backwards.

Rhythmic counterpoint. Two or more clearly-defined and independent rhythms played together.

Riff. In jazz, pop and rock, a short, memorable melodic pattern repeated many times in succession. See also **Ostinato**.

Ritornelle. French spelling of the Italian ritornello.

Ritornello. An instrumental section in a baroque aria, or a section for a large string-ensemble in a baroque concerto. In some arias and concerto movements the same or similar musical materials are used in every appearance of the ritornello (like the refrain of a rondo).

Rock steady. A slowed-down version of **ska**. One feature of rock steady was that the bass guitar became more important, often playing a melody of its own, and was the loudest of the instrumental parts.

Rondo. A composition in which a passage of music heard at the start is repeated several times, the repeats being separated from each other by contrasting passages of music.

Root. In tonal music, the fundamental pitch of any chord built from superimposed thirds. The fundamental pitch of a dominant triad (chord V) is the fifth degree of the scale of the prevailing key. If the key is C major the root of chord V is G, no matter which of the three pitches of chord V (G, B or D) is the bass note.

Sampler. A device for recording sections of sound (samples) as digital information. It allows them to be played back with various modifications (eg at different speeds, in continuous loops or in combination with other samples).

Samvadi. The second most strongly emphasised note in an Indian **rāg**. The samvadi is usually pitched a 4th or 5th away from the **vadi** (the most strongly emphasised note of a rāg).

Sarod. A north-Indian plucked-string instrument with a number of melody strings, drone strings and sympathetic strings. Unlike the sitar it has a metal fingerboard and no frets.

Scalic. An adjective referring to a melodic contour in which adjacent notes move by step in a similar manner to notes in a scale.

Scansion. The metre of verse.

Score. A written document representing how a piece of music should be played or how it was played.

Scotch snap. A two-note rhythm consisting of a short on-beat note followed by a long off-beat note (eg an on-beat semiquaver followed by an off-beat dotted quaver).

Scratching. The technique of manipulating a vinyl record in order to repeat a passage of music several times.

Semitone. The interval between two adjacent pitches on a keyboard instrument (including black notes). The semitone is the smallest interval in common use in western music.

Sequence. 1. The immediate repetition of a motif or phrase of a melody in the same part but at a different pitch. A harmonic progression can be treated in the same way. **2.** Performance data stored by a **sequencer**.

Sequencer. Computer software (or more rarely a purpose-built electronic device) for the input, editing and playback of music performance data using MIDI.

Serial music. Music based on manipulations of a series of 12 notes including every pitch of a chromatic scale.

Series. See **Tone row**.

Setting. Music added to a text so that the words are sung instead of spoken.

Seventh chord. A triad plus a note a 7th above the root. The dominant 7th consists of a major triad on the fifth degree of the scale (eg G–B–D in C major) plus a minor 7th above the root (F). In the same key the tonic 7th consists of a major triad on the first degree of the scale (C–E–G) plus a major 7th above the root (B).

Sextet. A composition for six instrumentalists or singers (or a mixture of both).

Sharp. 1. A sign (♯) that raises the pitch of a note a semitone. One or more sharp signs at the beginning of a stave make a key signature. Each sharp in a key signature raises notes with the same letter name by a semitone throughout the rest of the stave. A sharp inserted immediately in front of a note is an accidental, and its effect only lasts until the end of the bar. **2.** An adjective describing a note that is sung or played at a higher pitch than it should be.

Sitar. A north-Indian fretted plucked-string instrument, with a number of melody strings, drone strings and sympathetic strings.

Ska. A type of fast Afro-Caribbean pop music with strong off-beat accents.

Skank style. In guitar playing, a technique that involves chords being first struck sharply, then immediately dampened with the palm of the hand to abruptly cut off the sound.

Slendro. A pentatonic tuning system used in Indonesian gamelan music.

Solo. 1. A performance by a single musician. **2.** A piece of music or a passage of music written for a single musician.

Sonata. An instrumental composition, usually in several movements or sections, written for a single instrument or a small ensemble.

Sonata form. A musical structure consisting of three sections. In the first (exposition) a passage in the tonic key is contrasted with a passage in a different key. In the second (development) a wider range of keys lead back to a repeat of the first section (**recapitulation**), this time remaining in or close to the tonic key. From the early 19th century on the **coda** was often expanded to become an important fourth section.

Soprano. A high female or unbroken boy's voice.

Spiritual. An African-American folk song with a religious text.

Stave. Parallel lines on which pitches are notated.

Stem. The vertical line attached to the note-heads of time values shorter than a semibreve.

Step. As used in Great Britain, a **semitone** or **tone**. In America it means a tone (a semitone being a half step).

Strophic song. A song in which the same music is used for every verse.

Subdominant. The fourth degree of a major or minor scale (for example C in the key of G major).

Substitution chord. In jazz, a complex, chromatic and/or dissonant chord that has the same tonal function as the simple chord it replaces.

Suite. A collection of pieces intended to be performed together. In the baroque suite a number of dances in binary form and all in the same key were grouped together to form the dance suite. Later suites could consist of a series of extracts from an opera, ballet or musical.

Suling. A bamboo flute played in Javanese gamelan.

Swing quavers, swung quavers. The division of the beat into pairs of notes in which the first is longer than the second. In music notation this approximates to the ♩♪ pattern.

Symphony. As most often used today, an orchestral composition, often in four movements.

Syncopation. Accentuation of notes sounded off the beat or on a weak beak, often with rests on some of the strong beats.

Synthesiser. An electronic instrument that can produce and modify sound. It can be used to imitate other musical instruments and to produce non-musical sounds.

System. Two or more staves joined by a bracket at the left.

Tabla. 1. In Indian music, a pair of drums played with hands and fingers by a single performer. **2.** The smaller drum of this pair (the larger being called a **baya**).

Tāl (tala). A cyclic pattern in Indian music that forms the basis for rhythmic improvisation.

Talking drums. In Africa, drums on which a variety of sounds similar to elements of speech can be played and used for wordless communication.

Tanpura, tambura. A type of Indian plucked-string instrument with four drone strings.

Tape loop. A section of magnetic tape fixed end to end so that the same music can be repeated indefinitely. The process is now usually accomplished using a digital sequencer.

Tenor. A male voice higher than a bass, but lower than an alto.

Ternary form. A three-part structure (ABA) in which the first and last sections are identical or very similar. These enclose a contrasting central section.

Texture. The number and timbres of parts in a composition and the way they relate to each other.

Theorbo. A lute with very long unstopped strings allowing an extended bass range which makes it an ideal continuo instrument.

Through composed. A song in which new music is composed for each verse.

Timbre. The tone colour of an instrument or voice.

Time signature. Two numbers, one on top of the other, on a stave. The upper number usually indicates the number of beats per bar and the lower number indicates the time value of the beat.

Tirade. A very fast scalic flourish in baroque music.

Tonal music. Music based in a clearly defined key. A **key** is established by the relationships between the pitches of major and minor scales. The most important relationship is that between the tonic (the first degree of a scale) and all other pitches.

Tone. 1. An interval of two semitones, eg C–D. **2.** A sound of definite pitch. **3.** The timbre of a particular instrument or voice.

Tone row. A series of 12 different pitch classes. In strict serialism none of these pitch classes is repeated until all 12 have been used.

Tonic. The first degree of a major or minor scale.

Tonic pedal. The first degree of a scale held or repeated against changing harmony.

Transposition. The performance or notation of a passage of music or of a whole piece at a pitch level lower or higher than the original.

Treble. An unbroken boy's voice.

Triad. A chord of three pitches consisting of a bass note and notes a 3rd and a 5th above it.

Trio. 1. Music for three solo performers. **2.** Music for a single performer written throughout in three contrapuntal parts. **3.** The middle section of the minuet–trio–minuet group that forms the third movement of many classical symphonies and string quartets.

Trio sonata. A baroque composition in several sections or movements. It is usually printed on three staves and performed by two treble melody instruments, a bass melody instrument and one or more harmony instruments.

Tritone. An interval of three tones, eg F–B.

Tutti. A passage in which all or most of the members of an ensemble are playing.

Twelve-bar blues. A structure that originated in blues songs which has been widely adopted in jazz and pop music. The melody, which usually includes blue notes, consists of three four-bar phrases, the second often being a repeat of the first. The chord structure is built around chords I and IV and often takes the form I–I–I–I: IV–IV–I–I: V–IV–I–I (one chord per bar). Other patterns are possible (such as V–V–I–I for the last four bars) and chords are frequently decorated with 7ths or other additions.

Twelve-tone music. See **serial music**.

Unison. The combined sound of two or more notes of the same pitch.

Vadi. The most strongly emphasised note of an Indian rāg.

Variations. A musical structure in which a theme is repeated, each time with alterations to one or more of its original elements.

Verse and chorus. A standard form used in popular song in which a chorus is repeated after each verse. Sometimes an instrumental **break** or a **middle eight** is featured.

Viol, viola da gamba (Italian). Any of a family of bowed and fretted string instruments tuned like lutes and popular both as solo and accompanimental instruments throughout the 16th, 17th and early 18th centuries. The term *viola da gamba* (or just *gamba*) is often used nowadays to mean the bass viol.

Virtuoso. A performer of outstanding technical brilliance.